1996   No. 322

FAMILY PROCEEDINGS

SUPREME COURT

COUNTY COURTS

The Family Proceedings Rules (Northern Ireland) 1996

Made	*19th July 1996*
Coming into operation . .	*4th November 1996*
To be laid before Parliament	

We, the Family Proceedings Rules Committee, in exercise of the powers conferred on us by Article 12 of the Family Law (Northern Ireland) Order 1993(**a**), hereby with the concurrence of the Lord Chancellor, make the following Rules:—

PART I

PRELIMINARY

Citation and commencement

1.1. These Rules may be cited as the Family Proceedings Rules (Northern Ireland) 1996 and shall come into operation on 4th November 1996.

Revocation and saving

1.2.—(1) Subject to paragraph (2) the rules specified in paragraph (3) are hereby revoked.

(2) Nothing in these rules shall affect any proceedings which are pending (within the meaning of paragraph 1 of Schedule 8 to the Order of 1995) immediately before these rules come into operation and the rules in operation immediately before that day shall continue to apply to those proceedings.

(3) The rules referred to in paragraph (1) are

— the Matrimonial Causes Rules (Northern Ireland) 1981(**b**);

— the Matrimonial Causes (Amendment) Rules (Northern Ireland) 1989(**c**); and

---

(**a**)   S.I. 1993/1576 (N.I. 6)
(**b**)   S.R. 1981 No. 184
(**c**)   S.R. 1989 No. 246

— the Matrimonial Causes (Amendment) Rules (Northern Ireland) 1993(**a**).

Interpretation

1.3.—(1) In these Rules, unless the context otherwise requires—

"the Order of 1978" means the Matrimonial Causes (Northern Ireland) Order 1978(**b**);

"the Order of 1989" means the Matrimonial and Family Proceedings (Northern Ireland) Order 1989(**c**);

"the Order of 1991" means the Child Support (Northern Ireland) Order 1991(**d**);

"the Order of 1995" means the Children (Northern Ireland) Order 1995(**e**);

"ancillary relief" means—

    (*a*) an avoidance of disposition order,

    (*b*) a financial provision order,

    (*c*) an order for maintenance pending suit,

    (*d*) a property adjustment order, or

    (*e*) a variation order;

"avoidance of disposition order" means an order under Article 39(2)(*b*) or (*c*) of the Order of 1978;

"Board" means a Health and Social Services Board;

"business day" means any day other than a Saturday, a Sunday, Christmas Day, Good Friday or a bank holiday which is, or is to be observed as, a bank holiday in Northern Ireland under the Banking and Financial Dealings Act 1971(**f**);

"cause" means a matrimonial cause under the Order of 1978;

"certificate of readiness" means a certificate under rule 2.28;

"chief clerk" means the chief clerk for the county court division in which proceedings are pending;

"child" and "child of the family" have, except in Part IV, the same meanings, respectively assigned to them by Article 2(2) of the Order of 1978;

"consent order" means an order under Article 35A of the Order of 1978;

"county court office" means the office of the chief clerk for the county court division in which proceedings are pending;

"court" means the judge or the Master;

"defended cause" means a cause not being an undefended cause;

(**a**) S.R. 1993 No. 134
(**b**) S.I. 1978/1045 (N.I. 5)
(**c**) S.I. 1989/677 (N.I. 6)
(**d**) S.I. 1991/2628 (N.I. 23)
(**e**) S.I. 1995/755 (N.I. 2)
(**f**) 1971 c. 80

"Department" means the Department of Health and Social Services;

"divorce county court" means a county court so designated by the Lord Chancellor pursuant to Article 48(1) of the Order of 1978;

"document exchange" means any document exchange for the time being approved by the Lord Chancellor;

"family proceedings" means any proceedings with respect to which rules may be made under Article 12 of the Family Law (Northern Ireland) Order 1993;

"financial provision order" means any of the orders mentioned in Article 23(1) of the Order of 1978 except an order under Article 29(6) of that Order;

"financial relief" has the same meaning as in Article 39 of the Order of 1978;

"judge" means—

(a) in relation to proceedings in the High Court, a judge of the High Court; and

(b) in relation to proceedings in a county court, a county court judge;

"Master" means—

(a) in relation to proceedings in the High Court, the Master (Probate and Matrimonial) or the Master (Care and Protection) as the case may be; and

(b) in relation to proceedings in a county court, a district judge;

"Matrimonial Office" means the Probate and Matrimonial Office of the Supreme Court of Judicature of Northern Ireland;

"matrimonial proceedings" means subject to rule 2.4 any proceedings under the Order of 1978;

"notice of intention to defend" has the meaning assigned to it by rule 2.11;

"Office of Care and Protection" means the Office of Care and Protection of the Supreme Court of Judicature of Northern Ireland;

"person named" includes a person described as "passing under the name of A.B.";

"proper officer" means the proper officer of the High Court;

"property adjustment order" means an order under Article 26(1) of the Order of 1978;

"sealed copy" means a copy examined against the original, marked as examined by the examining officer and sealed with the appropriate seal;

"taxing master" means—

(a) in relation to proceedings in the High Court, the Master (Taxing Office); and

(b) in relation to proceedings in a county court, a district judge;

"Trust" means a Health and Social Services Trust by whom a function is exercisable by virtue of an authorisation for the time being in operation under Article 3(1) of the Health and Personal Social Services (Northern Ireland) Order 1994(**a**);

"undefended cause" means—

(*a*) in the case of an application under Article 16 of the Order of 1978, a cause in which the respondent has not given notice of intention to defend within the time limited, or

(*b*) in any other case—

    (i) a cause in which no answer has been filed or any answer filed has been struck out, or

    (ii) a cause which is proceeding only on the respondent's answer and in which no reply or answer to the respondent's answer has been filed or any such reply or answer has been struck out, or

    (iii) a cause to which rule 2.14(3) applies and in which no notice has been given under that rule or any notice so given has been withdrawn, or

    (iv) a cause in which an answer has been filed claiming relief but in which no pleading has been filed opposing the granting of a decree on the petition or answer or any pleading or part of a pleading opposing the granting of a decree;

"variation order" means an order under Article 33 of the Order of 1978(**b**);

(2) Unless the context otherwise requires, a cause may be treated as pending for the purpose of these Rules notwithstanding that a final decree or order has been pronounced or made on the petition.

(3) In these Rules a form referred to by number means the form so numbered in Appendix 1 or a form substantially to the like effect, with such variations as the circumstances of the particular case may require.

(4) In these Rules any reference to an Order and rule is—

(*a*) if prefixed by the letters "R.S.C.", a reference to that Order and rule in the Rules of the Supreme Court (Northern Ireland) 1980(**c**), and

(*b*) if prefixed by the letters "C.C.R.", a reference to that Order and rule in the County Court Rules (Northern Ireland) 1981(**d**).

(5) Unless the context otherwise requires, any reference in these Rules to any rule or statutory provision shall be construed as a reference to that rule or statutory provision as amended, extended or applied by any other rule or statutory provision.

(6) In these Rules any reference to a county court shall, in relation to matrimonial proceedings, be construed as a reference to a divorce county court.

(**a**) S.I. 1994/429 (N.I. 2)
(**b**) Article 33 was amended by Article 9 of the Matrimonial and Family Proceedings (Northern Ireland) Order 1989 (S.I. 1989/677 (N.I. 4))
(**c**) S.R. 1980 No. 346
(**d**) S.R. 1981 No. 225

Application of other rules

1.4.—(1) Subject to the provisions of these Rules and of any statutory provision, the Rules of the Supreme Court (Northern Ireland) 1980 and the County Court Rules (Northern Ireland) 1981 other than C.C.R. Order 25, rule 20 (which deals with a new hearing and rehearing) shall apply with the necessary modifications to the commencement of family proceedings in, and to the practice and procedure in family proceedings pending in, the High Court and a county court respectively.

(2) For the purpose of paragraph (1) any provision of these Rules authorising or requiring anything to be done in family proceedings shall be treated as if it were, in the case of proceedings pending in the High Court, a provision of the Rules of the Supreme Court (Northern Ireland) 1980 and in the case of proceedings pending in a county court, a provision of the County Court Rules (Northern Ireland) 1981.

PART II

MATRIMONIAL CAUSES

PETITION, PLEADINGS AND AMENDMENT

Application for leave to present a petition for nullity

2.1.—(1) An application under Article 16(4) of the Order of 1978 for leave to institute proceedings for a decree of nullity after the expiration of 3 years from the date of the marriage shall be made to the court in which the applicant wishes to present the petition, by originating summons in Form M1.

(2) There shall be filed in support of the summons an affidavit by the applicant exhibiting a copy of the proposed petition and (unless otherwise directed by the court on an application made ex parte) a certificate of the marriage and stating—

(*a*) the grounds of the application;

(*b*) whether there has been any previous application under Article 16(4) of the Order of 1978;

(*c*) the date of birth of each of the parties.

(3) When the summons is issued it shall be made returnable for a fixed date before the judge in chambers.

(4) Unless the court otherwise directs, the summons shall be served on the respondent at least 14 clear days before the return date.

(5) The respondent may be heard without filing an affidavit.

(6) This Part of these Rules shall, so far as applicable, apply with the necessary modifications, to the application as if the originating summons were a petition and the applicant a petitioner.

Discontinuance before service of petition

2.2. Before a petition is served on any person, the petitioner may file a notice of discontinuance and the cause shall thereupon stand dismissed.

Cause to be begun by petition

2.3.—(1) Every cause other than an application under Article 16(4) of the Order of 1978 shall be begun by petition.

(2) Where a petition for divorce, nullity or judicial separation discloses that there is a minor child of the family who is under the age of 16 years or who is over that age and is receiving instruction at an educational establishment or undergoing training for a trade, profession or vocation, the petition shall be accompanied by a statement signed by the petitioner personally containing the information required by Form M4, to which shall be attached a copy of any medical report mentioned therein.

Contents of petition

2.4.—(1) Unless the court otherwise directs, every petition shall contain the information required by Appendix 2.

(2) A petitioner who, in reliance on section 7 or 8 of the Civil Evidence Act (Northern Ireland) 1971(**a**), intends to adduce evidence that a person—

(*a*) was convicted of an offence by or before a court in the United Kingdom or by a court-martial there or elsewhere, or

(*b*) was found guilty of adultery in matrimonial proceedings or was found or adjudged to be the father of a child in relevant proceedings before a court in the United Kingdom,

must include in his petition a statement of his intention with particulars of—

(i) the conviction, finding or adjudication and the date thereof,

(ii) the court or court-martial which made the conviction, finding or adjudication and, in the case of a finding or adjudication the proceedings in which it was made, and

(iii) the issue in the proceedings to which the conviction, finding or adjudication is relevant.

(3) In this rule "matrimonial proceedings" and "relevant proceedings" have the same meaning as in section 8(5) of the Civil Evidence Act (Northern Ireland) 1971.

Signing of petition

2.5. Every petition shall be signed by counsel if settled by him or, if not, by the petitioner's solicitor in his own name or the name of his firm, or by the petitioner if he sues in person.

Presentation of petition

2.6.—(1) A petition may be presented to the High Court or, other than a petition under Article 21 of the Order of 1978, to any divorce county court.

(2) Unless the court otherwise directs on an application made ex parte, a certificate of the marriage to which the cause relates together with the certificates of birth of any child of the family under the age of 18 shall be filed with the petition.

(**a**) 1971 c. 36 (N.I.)

(3) Where there is before the court a petition which has not been dismissed or otherwise disposed of by a final order, another petition by the same petitioner in respect of the same marriage shall not be presented without leave granted on an application made in the pending proceedings:

Provided that no such leave shall be required where it is proposed, after the expiration of the period of 2 years from the date of the marriage, to present a petition for divorce alleging such of the facts mentioned in Article 3(2) of the Order of 1978 as were alleged in a petition for judicial separation presented before the expiration of that period.

(4) Subject to paragraph (5), the petition shall be presented by filing it in the Matrimonial Office together with a notice in Form M5 with Form M6 attached addressed to the respondent and any co-respondent together with any statement and report required by rule 2.3(2).

(5) The petition and other documents specified in paragraph (4) may be presented at any county court office or at the office of the chief clerk at Enniskillen, for transmission to the Matrimonial Office for filing.

(6) C.C.R. Order 6, rule 10 (which deals with the service of petitions) shall not apply but on the filing of the petition the master shall—

(a) affix thereto the seal of the Matrimonial Office,

(b) enter the cause in the appropriate records, and

(c) annex to every copy of the petition for service a notice in Form M5 with Form M6 attached and shall also annex to the copy petition for service on a respondent the copy of any statement and report filed pursuant to paragraph (4) of this rule.

Conciliation

2.7.—(1) Where—

(a) a petition for divorce, nullity of marriage or judicial separation has been presented and service on the respondent of the petition has been effected or dispensed with, and

(b) there are children of the family to whom Article 44 of the Order of 1978 applies;

the Master shall inform the Department with a view to a reference to a suitably qualified person (hereinafter called "the conciliator") to consider the possibility of conciliating the parties to the marriage.

(2) Where a reference is made under this rule the conciliator, subject to the approval of the Master, may inspect the court file.

(3) This rule shall not prejudice the right of any party to lodge a certificate of readiness.

Parties

2.8.—(1) Subject to paragraph (2), where a petition alleges that the respondent has committed adultery, the person with whom the adultery is alleged to have been committed shall be made a co-respondent in the cause unless—

(*a*) that person is not named in the petition and, if the adultery is relied on for the purpose of Article 3(2)(*a*) of the Order of 1978, the petition contains a statement that his or her identity is not known to the petitioner, or

(*b*) the court otherwise directs.

(2) Where a petition alleges that the respondent has been guilty of rape upon a person named, then, notwithstanding anything in paragraph (1), that person shall not be made a co-respondent in the cause unless the court so directs.

(3) Where a petition alleges that the respondent has been guilty of improper conduct (other than adultery) with a person named, the court may direct that the person named be made a co-respondent in the cause, and for that purpose the Master may cause notice to be given to the petitioner and to any other party who has given notice of intention to defend of a date and time when the court will consider giving such a direction.

(4) An application for directions under paragraph (1) may be made ex parte if no notice of intention to defend has been given.

(5) Paragraphs (1) and (3) of this rule do not apply where the person named has died before the filing of the petition.

Service of petition

2.9.—(1) Subject to the provisions of this rule and rules 6.4 and 7.3 a sealed copy of every petition shall be served personally or by post on every respondent or co-respondent together with a copy of the notice in Form M5 with Form M6 attached and with any statement and report required by rule 2.3(2).

(2) Personal service shall in no case be effected by the petitioner himself.

(3) An application for leave to substitute for the modes of service prescribed by paragraph (1) some other mode of service, or to substitute for service notice of the proceedings by advertisement or otherwise, shall be made ex parte by lodging with the Master an affidavit setting out the grounds on which the application is made.

(4) No order giving leave to substitute notice of the proceedings by advertisement shall be made unless it appears to the Master that there is a reasonable probability that the advertisement will come to the knowledge of the person concerned.

(5) Where leave is given to substitute for service notice of the proceedings by advertisement, the form of the advertisement shall be settled by the Master and copies of the newspapers containing the advertisement shall be filed.

(6) Where in the opinion of the Master it is impracticable to serve a party in accordance with any of the foregoing paragraphs or it is otherwise necessary or expedient to dispense with service of a copy of a petition on the respondent or on any other person, the Master may make an order dispensing with such service.

(7) An application for an order under paragraph (6) shall, if no notice of intention to defend has been given, be made in the first instance ex parte by lodging an affidavit setting out the grounds of the application, but the Master may, if he thinks fit, require the attendance of the petitioner on the application.

(8) Where the solicitor for the respondent or co-respondent signs a receipt that he accepts service of the petition on behalf of the party, the petition shall be deemed to have been duly served on that party and to have been so served on the date on which the receipt was signed.

Proof of service

2.10.—(1) A petition shall be deemed to be duly served if—

(*a*) an acknowledgement of service in Form M6 is signed by the party to be served or by a solicitor on his behalf and is returned to the Matrimonial Office, and

(*b*) where the form purports to be signed by the respondent, his signature is proved at the hearing.

(2) Where a copy of a petition has been sent to a party and no acknowledgement of service has been returned to the Matrimonial Office, the Master, if satisfied by affidavit or otherwise that the party has nevertheless received the document, may direct that the document shall be deemed to have been duly served on him.

(3) Where a copy of a petition has been served on a party personally and no acknowledgement of service has been returned to the Matrimonial Office, service shall be proved by filing an affidavit of service in Form M7 showing the server's means of knowledge of the identify of the party served.

(4) Where a solicitor has accepted service of a petition in accordance with rule 2.9(8), a copy of his receipt accepting service of the petition shall be lodged in the Matrimonial Office.

(5) Where an acknowledgement of service is returned to the Matrimonial Office, the proper officer shall send a photographic copy thereof to the solicitor for the petitioner or to the petitioner if he sues in person.

Notice of intention to defend

2.11.—(1) In these Rules any reference to a notice of intention to defend is a reference to an acknowledgement of service in Form M6 containing a statement to the effect that the person by whom or on whose behalf it is signed intends to defend the proceedings to which the acknowledgement relates, and any reference to giving notice of intention to defend is a reference to returning such a notice to the Matrimonial Office.

(2) In relation to any person on whom there is served a document requiring or authorising an acknowledgement of service to be returned to the Matrimonial Office references in these Rules to the time limited for giving notice of intention to defend are references to 14 days after service of the document, inclusive of the day of service, or such other time as may be fixed.

(3) Subject to paragraph (2), a person may give notice of intention to defend notwithstanding that he has already returned to the Matrimonial Office an acknowledgement of service not constituting such a notice.

Consent to the grant of a decree

2.12.—(1) Where, before the hearing of a petition alleging 2 years' separation coupled with the respondent's consent to a decree being granted, the respondent wishes to indicate to the court that he consents to the grant of a decree, he must do so by giving the Master a notice to that effect signed by the respondent personally.

For the purposes of this paragraph an acknowledgement of service containing a statement that the respondent consents to the grant of a decree shall be treated as such a notice if the acknowledgement is signed—

(*a*) in the case of a respondent acting in person, by the respondent, or

(*b*) in the case of a respondent represented by a solicitor, by the respondent as well as by the solicitor.

(2) A respondent to a petition which alleges any such fact as is mentioned in paragraph (1) may give notice to the court either that he does not consent to a decree being granted or that he withdraws any consent which he has already given.

Where any such notice is given and none of the other facts mentioned in Article 3(2) of the Order of 1978 is alleged, the proceedings on the petition shall be stayed and the Master shall thereupon give notice of the stay to all parties.

Supplemental petition, pleadings and amendment of petition

2.13.—(1) A supplemental petition may be filed only with leave.

(2) A petition may be amended without leave before it is served but only with leave after it has been served.

(3) Subject to paragraph (4), an application for leave under this rule—

(*a*) may, if every opposite party consents in writing to the supplemental petition being filed or the petition being amended, be made ex parte by lodging in the Matrimonial Office the supplemental petition or a copy of the petition as proposed to be amended, together with the appropriate consent, and

(*b*) shall, in any other case, be made by summons to be served, unless the court otherwise directs, on every opposite party.

(4) The Master may, if he thinks fit, require an application for leave to be supported by an affidavit.

(5) An order granting leave shall—

(*a*) where any party has given notice of intention to defend, fix the time within which his answer must be filed or amended,

(*b*) where the order is made after the certificate of readiness has been lodged, provide for a stay of the hearing until after the certificate has been renewed.

(6) An amendment authorised to be made under this rule shall be made by filing a copy of the amended petition.

(7) Rules 2.5 and 2.8 shall apply to a supplemental or amended petition as they apply to the original petition.

(8) Unless the court otherwise directs, a copy of a supplemental or amended petition, together with a copy of the order (if any) made under this rule shall be served on every respondent and co-respondent named in the original petition or in the supplemental or amended petition.

(9) Rules 2.9 and 2.10 shall apply to a respondent or co-respondent named in the original petition or in the supplemental or amended petition as they apply in relation to a person required to be served with an original petition.

Filing of answer to petition

2.14.—(1) Subject to paragraph (2) and to rules 2.12, 2.16 and 2.35, a respondent or co-respondent who has given notice of intention to defend and who—

(a) wishes to defend the petition or to dispute any of the facts alleged in it,

(b) being the respondent wishes to make in the proceedings any charge against the petitioner in respect of which the respondent prays for relief, or

(c) being the respondent to a petition to which Article 7(1) of the Order of 1978 applies, wishes to oppose the grant of a decree on the ground mentioned in that paragraph,

shall within 21 days after the expiration of the time limited for giving notice of intention to defend, file an answer to the petition.

(2) An answer may be filed at any time before the certificate of readiness has been lodged, notwithstanding that the time for filing the answer has expired.

(3) Where in a cause in which relief is sought under Article 14(d) of the Order of 1978 the respondent files an answer containing no more than a simple denial of the facts stated in the petition, he shall, if he intends to rebut the charges in the petition, give the proper officer notice to that effect either when filing his answer or later by leave of the court.

(4) On the filing of an answer to a petition presented to a divorce county court the Master shall order the cause to be transferred to the High Court, unless it is a case to which paragraph (3) applies and the respondent has not given any such a notice as is mentioned in that paragraph.

Filing of reply and subsequent pleadings

2.15.—(1) A petitioner may file a reply to an answer within 14 days after he has received a copy of the answer pursuant to rule 2.19.

(2) If the petitioner does not file a reply to an answer, he shall, unless the answer prays for a decree, be deemed on lodging the certificate of readiness to have denied every material allegation of fact made in the answer.

(3) No pleadings subsequent to a reply shall be filed without leave.

Filing of pleadings after lodgment of certificate of readiness

2.16. No pleadings shall be filed without leave after the certificate of readiness has been lodged.

Contents of answer and subsequent pleadings

2.17.—(1) Where an answer, reply or subsequent pleading contains more than a simple denial of the facts stated in the petition, answer or reply, as the case may be, the pleading shall set out with sufficient particularity the facts relied on but not the evidence by which they are to be proved and, if the pleading is filed by the husband or wife, it shall in relation to those facts, contain the information required in the case of a petition by paragraph 1(*m*) of Appendix 2.

(2) Unless the court otherwise directs, an answer by a husband or wife who disputes any statement required by paragraph 1(*f*), (*g*) and (*h*) of Appendix 2 to be included in the petition shall contain full particulars of the facts relied on.

(3) Paragraph 4(*a*) of Appendix 2 shall, where appropriate, apply, with the necessary modifications, to a respondent's answer as it applies to a petition.

Provided that it shall not be necessary to include in the answer any claim for costs against the petitioner.

(4) Where an answer to any petition contains a prayer for relief, it shall contain the information required by paragraph 1(1) of Appendix 2 in the case of the petition insofar as it has not been given by the petitioner.

(5) Rule 2.4(2) shall apply, with the necessary modifications, to a pleading other than a petition as it applies to a petition.

(6) Where a party's pleading includes such a statement as is mentioned in rule 2.4(2), then if the opposite party—

(*a*) denies the conviction, finding or adjudication to which the statement relates, or

(*b*) alleges that the conviction, finding or adjudication was erroneous, or

(*c*) denies that the conviction, finding or adjudication is relevant to any issue in the proceedings,

he must make the denial or allegation in his pleading.

(7) Rule 2.5 shall apply, with the necessary modifications, to a pleading other than a petition as it applies to a petition.

Allegation against third person in pleading

2.18.—(1) Rules 2.8, 2.9 and 2.10 shall apply, with the necessary modifications, to a pleading other than a petition as they apply to a petition, so however that for the references in those rules to a co-respondent there shall be substituted references to a party cited.

(2) Rule 2.14 shall apply, with the necessary modifications, to a party cited as it applies to a co-respondent.

Service of pleadings

2.19. A party who files an answer, reply or subsequent pleading shall within 7 days of filing it serve a copy thereof on every opposite party.

Supplemental answer and amendment of pleadings

2.20. Rule 2.13 shall apply, with the necessary modifications, to the filing of a supplemental answer, and the amendment of a pleading or other document not being a petition, as it applies to the filing of a supplemental petition and the amendment of a petition.

Service and amendment of pleadings

2.21. Pleadings in matrimonial proceedings may be served on any day except Sunday, Good Friday and Christmas Day and may be amended on any day on which the appropriate court office is open.

Particulars

2.22.—(1) A party on whom a pleading has been served may by notice request the party whose pleading it is to give particulars of any allegation or other matter pleaded and, if that party fails to give the particulars within a reasonable time the party requiring them may apply for an order that the particulars be given.

(2) A party giving particulars whether in pursuance of an order or otherwise shall at the same time file a copy of them.

Re-transfer of cause to divorce county court

2.23.—(1) Where a cause begun by petition has been transferred to the High Court under rule 2.14(4) and subsequently becomes undefended, the court shall order it to be re-transferred to a divorce county court, unless, (because of the proximity of the probable date of trial or for any other reason) the court thinks it desirable that the cause should be heard and determined in the High Court.

(2) Nothing in paragraph (1) shall require a case to be re-transferred at the time when it becomes undefended if in the opinion of the court the question whether it is desirable to retain it in the High Court cannot conveniently be considered until later.

PREPARATION FOR TRIAL

Discovery of documents

2.24. A party to a cause may apply for an order for discovery and inspection of documents by an opposite party and R.S.C. Order 24 shall apply with the necessary modifications.

Discovery by interrogatories

2.25.—(1) R.S.C. Order 26 (which deals with discovery by interrogatories) shall apply to a cause with the necessary modifications.

(2) A copy of the proposed interrogatories shall be filed when the summons for an order is issued.

Medical examination in proceedings for nullity

2.26.—(1) In proceedings for nullity on the grounds of incapacity to consummate the marriage the petitioner may apply to the Master to determine whether medical inspectors should be appointed to examine the parties.

(2) An application under paragraph (1) shall not be made in an undefended cause—

(*a*) if the husband is the petitioner, or

(*b*) if the wife is the petitioner and—

   (i) it appears from the petition that she was either a widow or divorced at the time of marriage in question, or

   (ii) it appears from the petition or otherwise that she has borne a child, or

   (iii) a statement by the wife that she is not a virgin is filed,

unless, in any such case, the petitioner is alleging his or her own incapacity.

(3) References in paragraph (1) and (2) to the petitioner shall, where the cause is proceeding only on the respondent's answer or where the allegation of incapacity is made only in the respondent's answer, be construed as references to the respondent.

(4) An application under paragraph (1) by the petitioner shall be made—

(*a*) where the respondent has not given notice of intention to defend, after the time limited for giving notice of intention to defend has expired;

(*b*) where the respondent has given notice of intention to defend, after the expiration of the time allowed for filing his answer or, if he has filed an answer, after it has been filed;

and any application under paragraph (1) by the respondent shall be made after he has filed an answer.

(5) Where the party required to make an application under paragraph (1) fails to do so within a reasonable time, the other party may, if he is prosecuting or defending the cause, make the application.

(6) In proceedings for nullity on the ground that the marriage has not been consummated owing to the wilful refusal of the respondent, either party may apply to the Master for the appointment of medical inspectors to examine the parties.

(7) If the respondent has not given notice of intention to defend, an application by the petitioner under paragraph (1) or (6) may be made ex parte.

(8) If the Master hearing an application under paragraph (1) or (6) considers it expedient to do so, he shall appoint a medical inspector or, if he thinks it necessary, two medical inspectors to examine the parties and report to the court the result of the examination.

(9) At the hearing of any such proceedings as are referred to in paragraph (1) the court may, if it thinks fit, appoint a medical inspector or two medical inspectors to examine any party who has not been examined or to examine further any party who has been examined.

(10) The party on whose application an order under paragraph (8) is made or who has the conduct of proceedings in which an order under paragraph (9) has been made for the examination of the other party, shall serve on the other party notice of the time and place appointed for his or her examination.

Conduct of medical examination

2.27.—(1) The examination under rule 2.26 shall, if either party so requires, be held at the residence of one of the medical inspectors appointed or at some other convenient place selected by them and in every other case shall be held at the Matrimonial Office.

(2) Where a medical inspection takes place at a place other than the Matrimonial Office every party presenting himself for examination shall sign, in the presence of the inspector or inspectors, a statement that he is the person referred to as the petitioner or respondent, as the case may be, in the order for the examination, and at the conclusion of the examination the inspector or inspectors shall certify on the statement that it was signed in his or their presence by the person who has been examined. Where the medical inspection takes place in the Matrimonial Office the identification shall be conducted before the Master in such manner as he may direct.

(3) Every report made in pursuance of rule 2.26 shall be filed and either party shall be entitled to be supplied with a copy on payment of the prescribed fee.

(4) It shall not be necessary in any cause for the inspector or inspectors to attend or give evidence at the trial unless required either by the court of its own motion or by either party to do so after receiving appropriate notice.

(5) Where pursuant to paragraph (4) the evidence of the inspector or inspectors is not given at the trial, his or their report shall be treated as information furnished to the court by a court expert and be given such weight as the court thinks fit.

Entry for hearing and certificate of readiness

2.28.—(1) The petitioner or any party who is defending a cause or the respondent in the case of an undefended cause proceeding on the respondent's answer may request the Master to enter the cause for hearing if—

(*a*) a copy of the petition (including any supplemental or amended petition) and any subsequent pleading has been duly served on every party requiring to be served and, where that party is a person under disability, any affidavit required by rule 6.4(2) has been filed;

(*b*) (i) no notice of intention to defend has been given by any party entitled to defend and the time limited for giving such notice has expired; or

(ii) where a notice of intention to defend has been given by any party, the time allowed for filing an answer has expired; or

(iii) where an answer has been filed, the time allowed for filing any subsequent pleading has expired;

(*c*) in proceedings for nullity, where an order for the examination of the parties has been made on an application under rule 2.26, the notice required by paragraph 10 of that rule has been served and the report of the inspector or inspectors has been filed;

(*d*) any other directions of the court have been complied with.

(2) The party making such request shall at the same time lodge in the Matrimonial Office a certificate in Form M8 that the cause is ready for trial and, in the case of a cause for hearing in a divorce county court, the certificate shall state the place of trial requested.

(3) The party lodging the certificate of readiness shall at the same time deliver to the Matrimonial Office a bundle of pleadings for the judge consisting of an indexed copy of the following documents—

(*a*) the certificate of readiness;

(*b*) the petition;

(*c*) any other pleadings;

(*d*) notices for particulars and answers thereto;

(*e*) affidavit of service;

(*f*) interlocutory orders;

(*g*) any statement as to arrangements for children under rule 2.3(2);

(*h*) any statement under rule 2.29(4);

(*i*) the requisite legal aid documents,

fastened together in the order shown and having endorsed thereon the names and addresses of the solicitors of the parties.

(4) If there are any further proceedings after the lodging of the certificate of readiness, the party lodging the certificate shall deliver to the proper officer or the chief clerk, as the case may be, for the use of the judge a copy of any further document of the kind mentioned in paragraph (3).

Stay under Schedule 1 to the Order of 1978

2.29.—(1) An application to the court by the petitioner or respondent in proceedings for divorce for an order under paragraph 8 of Schedule 1 to the Order of 1978 (in this rule referred to as "Schedule 1") shall be made to the Master, who may determine the application or refer the application, or any question arising thereon, to the judge for his decision as if the application were an application for ancillary relief.

(2) An application for an order under paragraph 9 of Schedule 1 to the Order of 1978 shall be made to the judge.

(3) Where on the lodgment of the certificate of readiness, it appears to the Master from any information given pursuant to paragraph 1(1) of Appendix 2 or rule 2.17(4) or paragraph (4) of this rule that any proceedings which are in respect of the marriage in question or which are capable of affecting its validity or subsistence are continuing in any country outside Northern Ireland and he considers that the question whether the proceedings on the petition should be stayed under paragraph 9 of Schedule 1 ought to be

determined by the court, he shall before proceeding under rule 2.32 fix a date and time for the consideration of that question by the judge and give notice thereof to all parties.

In this paragraph "proceedings continuing in any country outside Northern Ireland" has the same meaning as in paragraph 1(1) of Appendix 2.

(4) Any party who lodges a certificate of readiness in matrimonial proceedings within the meaning of paragraph 2 of Schedule 1 shall, if there has been a change in the information given pursuant to paragraph 1(1) of Appendix 2 and rule 2.17(4), file a statement giving particulars of the change.

(5) An application by a party to the proceedings for an order under paragraph 10 of Schedule 1 to the Order of 1978 may be made to the Master, and he may determine the application or may refer the application, or any question arising thereon, to the judge as if the application were an application for ancillary relief.

TRIAL ETC

Mode and place of trial

2.30.—(1) Subject to section 62(4) of the Judicature (Northern Ireland) Act 1978(**a**), every cause and any issue arising therein shall be tried by a judge without a jury.

(2) A cause pending in a divorce county court may be heard at any county court sitting for any division but, subject to the provisions of rules 2.31 and 2.32, shall be heard at the place of trial requested in the certificate of readiness.

(3) Unless the judge otherwise directs, every cause listed for hearing and any issue arising therein shall be heard by a judge in chambers and adjourned into court for judgment.

Setting down for trial

2.31.—(1) A cause shall be deemed to have been set down as soon as the certificate of readiness has been lodged.

(2) Where a cause is set down for hearing in the High Court, the proper officer shall, as soon as practicable, fix the date of the hearing and give notice thereof to every party to the case.

(3) Where a cause is set down for hearing in a divorce county court, the proper officer shall forthwith send the file of the cause and the bundle of pleadings to the chief clerk.

(4) As soon as practicable after the chief clerk has received the file of the cause and the bundle of pleadings in accordance with paragraph (3), he shall fix the date and place of the hearing and give notice thereof to every party to the cause.

(5) Except with the consent of all parties or by leave of the judge, no cause shall be tried before the expiration of 10 days from the date of issue stamped on the notice of hearing.

(**a**) 1978 c. 23

Order for transfer of cause

2.32.—(1) A divorce county court may order that a cause pending therein be transferred to the High Court, if, having regard to all the circumstances including the difficulty or importance of the cause or of any issue arising therein, the court thinks it desirable that the cause should be heard and determined in the High Court.

(2) The court may, if it appears to it that a cause cannot conveniently be tried at the place of trial requested in accordance with rule 2.28(2), change the place of trial to another place within the same or another county court division.

(3) The power conferred by paragraph (2) may be exercised by the judge or Master of his own motion or on the application of a party, but before acting of his own motion the judge or Master shall give the parties an opportunity of being heard on the question of change, and for that purpose the chief clerk shall give the parties notice of the date and place at which the question will be considered.

Trial of issue

2.33. Where directions are given for the separate trial of any issue, the Master shall—

(*a*) if the issue arises on an application for ancillary relief or on an application with respect to any child or alleged child of the family, proceed as if the issue were a question referred to a judge on an application for ancillary relief and rule 2.70 shall apply accordingly.

(*b*) in any other case, cause the issue to be set down for trial.

Lists in the divorce county court

2.34.—(1) The chief clerk for each county court division shall maintain a list of the causes which are for the time being set down for trial in that division.

(2) Causes shall be entered in the said list in the order in which they were set down for trial and for the purpose of this paragraph—

(*a*) a cause shall, subject to sub-paragraph (*b*), be treated as having been set down for trial when the file of the cause is received by the chief clerk from the Matrimonial Office under rule 2.31(3);

(*b*) a cause transferred for trial from another county court division shall be treated as having been set down for trial at the end of the day on which it was originally set down for trial.

Right to be heard on ancillary questions

2.35.—(1) A respondent, co-respondent or party cited may, without filing an answer, be heard on any question as to costs or as to ancillary relief.

(2) A party shall be entitled to be heard on any question pursuant to paragraph (2) whether or not he has returned to the Matrimonial Office an acknowledgement of service stating his wish to be heard on that question.

18

(3) The court may at any time order any party objecting to a claim for costs to file and serve on the party making the claim a written statement setting out the reasons for his objection.

(4) In proceedings after a decree nisi of divorce or a decree of judicial separation no order the effect of which would be to make a co-respondent or party cited liable for costs which are not directly referable to the decree shall be made unless the co-respondent or party cited is a party to such proceedings or has been given notice of the intention to apply for such an order.

Respondent's statement as to arrangements for children

2.36.—(1) A respondent on whom there is served a statement in accordance with rule 2.3(2) may file in the Matrimonial Office a written statement of his views on the present and proposed arrangements for the children, and on receipt of such a statement from the respondent the proper officer shall send a copy to the petitioner.

(2) Any such statement of the respondent's views shall, if practicable, be filed within the time limited for giving notice of intention to defend and in any event before the judge considers the arrangements or proposed arrangements for the children under Article 44 of the Order of 1978(**a**).

Procedure for complying with Article 44 of the Order of 1978

2.37.—(1) Where no such application as is referred to in rule 2.38(1) is pending the judge shall consider the matters specified in Article 44(1) of the Order of 1978 in accordance with the provisions of this rule.

(2) Where, on consideration of the relevant evidence, including any further evidence or report provided pursuant to this rule and any statement filed by the respondent under rule 2.36 the judge is satisfied that—

(*a*) there are no children of the family to whom Article 44 of the Order of 1978 applies, or

(*b*) there are such children but the court need not exercise its powers under the Order of 1995 with respect to any of them or give any directions under Article 44 of the Order of 1978,

the judge shall certify accordingly and, in a case to which sub-paragraph (*b*) applies, the petitioner and the respondent shall each be sent a copy of the certificate by the Master.

(3) Where the judge is not satisfied as mentioned in paragraph (2) above he may, without prejudice to his powers under the Order of 1995 or Article 44 of the Order of 1978, give one or more of the following directions—

(*a*) that the parties, or any of them, shall file further evidence relating to the arrangements for the children (and the direction shall specify the matters to be dealt with in the further evidence);

(*b*) that a welfare report on the children, or any of them be prepared;

(*c*) that the parties, or any of them, shall attend before him at the date, time and place specified in the direction;

and the parties shall be notified accordingly.

(**a**) S.I. 1978/1045 (N.I. 5) as substituted by paragraph 95 of Schedule 9 to the Children (Northern Ireland) Order 1995 (S.I. 1995/755 (N.I. 2))

(4) Where the court gives a direction under Article 44(2) of the Order of 1978 notice of the direction shall be given to the parties.

(5) In this rule 'parties' means the petitioner, the respondent and any person who appears to the court to have the care of the child.

Applications relating to children of the family

2.38.—(1) Where a cause is pending, an application by a party to the cause or by any other person for an order under Part II or Part III or Part XV of the Order of 1995 in relation to a child of the family shall be made in the cause; and where the applicant is not a party and has obtained such leave as is required under the Order of 1995 to make the application no leave to intervene in the cause shall be necessary.

(2) If, while a cause is pending, proceedings relating to any child of the family are begun in any other court, a concise statement of the nature of the proceedings shall forthwith be filed by the person beginning the proceedings, or if he is not a party to the cause by the petitioner.

Restoration of matters adjourned, etc at the hearing

2.39.—(1) Where at the trial of a cause any application is adjourned by the judge it may be restored by any party or by the Master when in his opinion the matter ought to be further considered, by notice in Form M9 which shall be served on every party concerned and (when served by a party) on the proper officer or chief clerk, as the case may be.

(2) Where in proceedings for divorce, nullity of marriage or judicial separation the judge has made a direction under Article 44(2) of the Order of 1978, paragraph (1) shall, unless the judge otherwise directs, apply as if an application with respect to the arrangements for the care and upbringing of any such child had been adjourned.

EVIDENCE

Evidence generally

2.40. Subject to the provisions of rules 2.41 and 2.42 and of the Civil Evidence Act (Northern Ireland) 1971(**a**) and any other statutory provisions, any fact required to be proved by the evidence of witnesses at the trial of a cause begun by petition shall be proved by the examination of the witnesses orally.

Evidence by affidavit, etc

2.41.—(1) The court may order—

(a) that any particular fact to be specified in the order may be proved by affidavit,

(b) that the affidavit of any witness may be read at the trial on such conditions as the court thinks reasonable,

---

(**a**) 1971 c. 36 (N.I.)

(*c*) that the evidence of any particular fact shall be given at the trial in such manner as may be specified in the order and in particular—

    (i) by statement on oath of information or belief, or

    (ii) by the production of documents or entries in books, or

    (iii) by copies of documents or entries in books, or

(*d*) that not more than a specified number of expert witnesses may be called.

(2) An application to the Master for an order under paragraph (1) shall—

(*a*) if no notice of intention to defend has been given, or

(*b*) if the petitioner and every party who has given notice of intention to defend consents to the order sought, or

(*c*) if the cause is undefended and the certificate of readiness has been lodged,

be made ex parte by filing an affidavit stating the grounds on which the application is made.

(3) Where an application is made before the trial for an order that the affidavit of a witness may be read at the trial or that evidence of a particular fact may be given at the trial by affidavit, the affidavit or a draft thereof shall be submitted with the application; and where the affidavit is sworn before the hearing of the application and sufficiently states the grounds on which the application is made, no other affidavit shall be required under paragraph (2).

(4) The court may, on the application of any party to a cause begun by petition, make an order for the examination on oath of any person, and R.S.C. Order 38, rule 7, and Order 39, rules 1 to 14, (which regulate the procedure where evidence is to be taken by deposition) shall have effect accordingly with the appropriate modifications.

(5) On any interlocutory application made to the court evidence may be given by affidavit unless these Rules otherwise provide or the court otherwise directs, but the court may, on the application of any party, order the attendance for cross-examination of the person making any such affidavit; and where, after such attendance has been ordered, such affidavit shall not be used as evidence without the leave of the court.

(6) Medical and other expert evidence or the evidence of an inquiry agent to prove adultery may without leave, and in an undefended cause shall, be given by affidavit, but the court may, of its own motion or on the application of any party at the trial, order the attendance for cross-examination of the person making any such affidavit; and after such attendance has been ordered such affidavit shall not be used in evidence without the leave of the court.

(7) Where the statement of a co-respondent or a person named admitting his or her adultery with the respondent or of a respondent admitting his or her adultery with a person named or a co-respondent has been made in the presence and hearing of the person with whom adultery is admitted, the affidavit must contain an averment that the statement has been so made.

Evidence of marriage outside Northern Ireland

2.42.—(1) The celebration of a marriage outside Northern Ireland and its validity under the law of the country where it was celebrated may, in any family proceedings in which the existence and validity of the marriage is not disputed, be proved by the evidence of one of the parties to the marriage and the production of a document purporting to be—

(*a*) a marriage certificate or similar document issued under the law in force in that country; or

(*b*) a certified copy of an entry in a register of marriages kept under the law in force in that country.

(2) Where a document produced by virtue of paragraph (1) is not in English it shall, unless the court otherwise directs, be accompanied by a translation certified by a notary public or authenticated by affidavit.

(3) This rule shall not be construed as precluding the proof of a marriage in accordance with the Evidence (Foreign, Dominion and Colonial Documents) Act 1933(**a**) or in any other manner authorised apart from this rule.

Rules 2.41 and 2.42 not to affect the power of the judge at the trial to refuse to admit any evidence

2.43. Nothing in rule 2.41 or 2.42 shall affect the power of the judge at the trial to refuse to admit any evidence if in the interest of justice he thinks fit to do so.

Issue of writ of subpoena or witness summons

2.44.—(1) A writ of subpoena in a cause pending in the High Court shall be issued out of the Matrimonial Office.

(2) A witness summons in a cause pending in a divorce county court shall be issued in any county court office.

Hearsay and expert evidence

2.45.—(1) R.S.C. Order 38, rules 5 and 19(1) shall not apply in relation to an undefended cause in the High Court.

(2) R.S.C. Order 38, rule 19 shall have effect in relation to a defended cause in the High Court as if—

(*a*) for the words "this Order" in paragraph (3), there were substituted a reference to rule 2.41 of these Rules; and

(*b*) paragraph (4) were omitted.

(3) Unless in any particular case the court otherwise directs, C.C.R. Order 38, rule 19(1), shall not apply in relation to an undefended cause pending in a divorce county court.

(**a**) 1933 c. 4

Decrees and orders

2.46.—(1) Every decree, every order made in open court and every other order which is required to be drawn up shall be drawn up—

(*a*) in the case of a decree or order pronounced or made in the High Court, in the Matrimonial Office;

(*b*) in the case of a decree or order pronounced or made in a divorce county court, in the county court office;

and shall have affixed thereto the seal of the office in which it is drawn up.

(2) C.C.R. Order 33, rule 4(1) (which deals with the lodgment of a decree) shall not apply to a decree pronounced in a cause pending in a divorce county court.

(3) The chief clerk to whom the file of a cause has been sent under rule 2.31(3) shall, as soon as practicable after the cause has been tried, forward to the Matrimonial Office a copy of the decree or order pronounced or made in the cause.

Application for rescission of decree

2.47.—(1) An application by a respondent under Article 12(1) of the Order of 1978 for the rescission of a decree of divorce shall be made to a judge and shall be heard in open court.

(2) Unless otherwise directed, the notice of the application shall be served on the petitioner not less than 14 days before the day fixed by the proper officer or chief clerk, as the case may be, for the hearing of the application.

(3) The applicant shall file an affidavit showing that the notice of the application has been served.

(4) The application shall be supported by an affidavit setting out the allegations on which the applicant relies and a copy of the affidavit shall be served on the petitioner.

Application under Article 12(2) of the Order of 1978

2.48.—(1) An application by the respondent to a petition for divorce for the court to consider his financial position after the divorce shall be made by notice in Form M14.

(2) Where a petitioner is served with a notice in Form M14, then, unless he has already filed an affidavit under rule 2.61(2), he shall, within 14 days after the service of the notice, file an affidavit in answer to the application containing full particulars of his property and income, and if he does not do so, the court may order him to file an affidavit containing such particulars.

(3) Within 14 days after service of any affidavit under paragraph (2) or within such other time as the court may fix, the respondent shall file an affidavit in reply containing full particulars of his property and income unless already given in an affidavit filed by him under rule 2.61(3).

(4) The powers of the court on the hearing of the application may be exercised by the Master.

(5) The Master by whom an application under Article 12(2) of the Order of 1978 is to be heard shall fix an appointment for the hearing, and rules 2.64(3) to (7); 2.68 and 2.69 shall apply to the application as if it were an application for ancillary relief.

(6) At any time before the hearing of the application is concluded (and without prejudice to any right of appeal), the Master may, and if so requested by either party shall, refer the application or any question arising thereon, to a judge.

(7) A statement of any of the matters mentioned in paragraph (3) of Article 12 of the Order of 1978 with respect to which the court is satisfied, a statement that the conditions for which that paragraph and paragraph (4) provide have been fulfilled, shall be entered in the court records.

Intervention to show cause by the Crown Solicitor

2.49.—(1) If the Crown Solicitor wishes to show cause why a decree nisi should not be made absolute, he shall give notice to that effect to the proper officer or chief clerk, as the case may be, and to the party in whose favour it was pronounced, and, if the cause is pending in a divorce county court, the Master shall thereupon order it to be transferred to the High Court.

(2) Within 21 days after giving notice under paragraph (1) the Crown Solicitor shall file his plea setting out the ground on which he desires to show cause, together with a copy for service on the party in whose favour the decree was pronounced and every other party affected by the decree.

(3) The proper officer shall serve a copy of the plea on each of the persons mentioned in paragraph (2).

(4) Except as hereinafter provided, these Rules shall apply to all subsequent pleadings and proceedings in respect of the plea as if it were a petition.

(5) If no answer to the plea is filed within the time limited, or if an answer is filed and is struck out or not proceeded with, the Crown Solicitor may apply forthwith by motion to rescind the decree nisi and dismiss the petition.

(6) If an answer is filed denying all the charges in the plea, the Crown Solicitor shall within 14 days thereafter request the proper officer to enter the intervention for hearing but, if no such request is made, the party in whose favour the decree nisi was pronounced may request the proper officer to enter the intervention for hearing or may apply under rule 2.52 to make the decree absolute.

(7) If an answer is filed in which any charge in the plea is not denied, the party in whose favour the decree nisi was pronounced may within 14 days after the answer has been filed request the proper officer to enter the intervention for hearing but, if no such request is made, the Crown Solicitor may apply forthwith by motion to rescind the decree and dismiss the petition.

(8) The Crown Solicitor or the party in whose favour the decree was pronounced, as the case may be shall, when requesting the intervention to be

24

entered for hearing, deliver to the Matrimonial Office a bundle of pleadings for the judge consisting of an indexed copy of the following documents:—

(*a*) the decree nisi;

(*b*) the Crown Solicitor's plea;

(*c*) the answer;

(*d*) notices for particulars and answers thereto;

(*e*) affidavits, if any;

(*f*) the requisite legal aid documents,

fastened together in the order shown and having endorsed thereon the names and addresses of the solicitors of the parties.

(9) After the expiration of 7 days from the date on which the proper officer was requested to enter the intervention for hearing, the intervention shall be deemed to be set down for trial and the proper officer shall—

(*a*) give notice to this effect to every party to the intervention, and

(*b*) as soon as practicable thereafter fix the date of the hearing and give notice thereof to every party to the intervention.

Intervention to show cause by person other than Crown Solicitor

2.50.—(1) If any person other than the Crown Solicitor wishes to show cause under Article 11 of the Order of 1978 why a decree nisi should not be made absolute, he shall file an affidavit stating the facts on which he relies and a copy shall be served on the party in whose favour the decree was pronounced.

(2) A party on whom a copy of an affidavit has been served under paragraph (1) may, within 14 days after service, file an affidavit in answer and, if he does so, a copy thereof shall be served on the person showing cause.

(3) The person showing cause may file an affidavit in reply within 14 days after service of the affidavit in answer and, if he does so, a copy shall be served on each party who was served with a copy of his original affidavit.

(4) No affidavit after an affidavit in reply shall be filed without leave.

(5) Any person who files an affidavit under paragraph (1), (2) or (3) shall at the same time file a copy for service on each person required to be served therewith and the proper officer or chief clerk, as the case may be, shall thereupon serve the copy on that person.

(6) A person showing cause shall apply to the judge for directions within 14 days after expiry of the time allowed for filing an affidavit in reply or, where no affidavit in answer has been filed, within 14 days after expiry of the time allowed for filing such an affidavit.

(7) If the person showing cause does not apply under paragraph (6) within the time limited, the person in whose favour the decree was pronounced may do so.

(8) The judge may either give directions for the trial of the intervention or, if he is satisfied that there is no question to be tried, dismiss the intervention.

(9) If the judge gives such directions in a cause pending in a divorce county court, he shall thereupon order the cause to be transferred to the High Court.

(10) When directions have been given under paragraph (8) and, if necessary, the cause has been transferred to the High Court, the intervention shall proceed as nearly as may be in the manner prescribed by paragraphs (6) to (9) of rule 2.49, substituting for references to the Crown Solicitor references to the person showing cause, but no plea or answer need be filed unless the judge so directs.

Rescission of decree nisi by consent

2.51.—(1) Where a reconciliation has been effected between the petitioner and the respondent—

(*a*) after a decree nisi has been pronounced but before it has been made absolute, or

(*b*) after the pronouncement of a decree of judicial separation,

either party may apply for an order rescinding the decree by consent.

(2) Where the cause is pending in a divorce county court, the application shall be made on notice to the other spouse and to any other party against whom costs have been awarded or who is otherwise affected by the decree, and where the cause is pending in the High Court, a copy of the summons by which the application is made shall be served on every such person.

(3) The application shall be made to the judge and shall be heard in chambers.

Decree absolute on lodging notice

2.52.—(1) Subject to rule 2.53(1), an application by a spouse to make absolute a decree nisi pronounced in his favour may be made by lodging with the proper officer or chief clerk, as the case may be, notice in Form M10.

(2) On the lodging of such a notice, the proper officer or chief clerk, as the case may be, shall search the court records and if he is satisfied—

(*a*) that no appeal against the decree and no application for rescission of the decree is pending;

(*b*) that no order has been made by the Court of Appeal extending the time for appealing against the decree or, if any such order has been made, that the time so extended has expired;

(*c*) that no application for such an order as is mentioned in sub-paragraph (*b*) is pending;

(*d*) that no intervention under rule 2.49 or 2.50 is pending;

(*e*) that the court has complied with Article 44(1) of the Order of 1978 and has not given any direction under Article 44(2);

(*f*) where a certificate has been granted under section 12 of the Administration of Justice Act 1969(**a**) in respect of the decree—

(**a**) 1969 c. 58

(i) that no application for leave to appeal directly to the House of Lords is pending;

(ii) that no extension of the time to apply for leave to appeal directly to the House of Lords has been granted or, if any such extension has been granted, that the time so extended has expired; and

(iii) that the time for any appeal to the Court of Appeal has expired; and

(g) that the provisions of Article 12(2) to (4) of the Order of 1978 do not apply or have been complied with,

the Master shall make the decree absolute.

Provided that if the notice is lodged more than 12 months after the decree nisi, the Master may require the applicant to file an affidavit accounting for the delay and may make the decree absolute if he thinks fit or refer the application to the judge.

Decree absolute on application

2.53.—(1) In the following cases an application for a decree nisi to be made absolute shall be made to the judge by summons, that is to say—

(a) where, within 6 weeks after a decree nisi has been pronounced, the Crown Solicitor gives to the proper officer or chief clerk, as the case may be, and to the party in whose favour the decree was pronounced a notice that he requires more time to decide whether to show cause against the decree being made absolute and the notice has not been withdrawn, or

(b) where there are other circumstances which in the opinion of the Master ought to be brought to the attention of the court before the decree nisi is made absolute.

Unless the court otherwise directs, the summons shall be served on every party to the cause (other than the applicant) and, in a case to which sub-paragraph (a) applies, on the Crown Solicitor.

(2) An application by a spouse for a decree nisi pronounced against him to be made absolute may be made to the judge or the Master by summons to be served on the other spouse not less than 7 clear days before the day on which the application is to be heard.

(3) An order granting an application under this rule shall not take effect until the proper officer or chief clerk, as the case may be, has searched the court records and is satisfied as to the matters mentioned in rule 2.52(2).

Indorsement and certificate of decree absolute

2.54.—(1) Where a decree nisi is made absolute, the Master shall make an indorsement to that effect on the decree, stating the precise time at which it was made absolute.

(2) On a decree nisi being made absolute, the proper officer or chief clerk, as the case may be, shall—

(*a*) send to the petitioner and the respondent a certificate in Form M11 or M12, authenticated by the appropriate seal, and

(*b*) if the cause is pending in a divorce county court, notify the Matrimonial Office.

(3) A certificate in Form M11 or M12 that a decree nisi has been made absolute shall be issued to any person requiring it on payment of the prescribed fee.

(4) A central index of decrees absolute shall be kept in the Matrimonial Office and any person shall be entitled to require a search to be made therein, and to be furnished with a certificate of the result of the search, on payment of the prescribed fee.

ANCILLARY RELIEF

Application by petitioner or respondent for ancillary relief

2.55.—(1) Any application by a petitioner or by a respondent who files an answer claiming relief, for—

(*a*) an order for maintenance pending suit,

(*b*) a financial provision order,

(*c*) a property adjustment order,

shall be made in the petition or answer, as the case may be.

(2) Notwithstanding anything in paragraph (1), an application for ancillary relief which should have been made in the petition or answer may be made subsequently—

(*a*) by leave of the court, either by notice in Form M13 or at the trial, or

(*b*) where the parties are agreed upon the terms of the proposed order, without leave by notice in Form M13.

(3) An application by a petitioner or respondent for ancillary relief, not being an application which is required to be made in the petition or answer, shall be made by notice in Form M13.

Application by parent, guardian etc for ancillary relief in respect of children

2.56.—(1) Any of the following persons, namely—

(*a*) a parent or guardian of any child of the family;

(*b*) any person in whose favour a residence order has been made with respect to a child of the family, and any applicant for such an order;

(*c*) any other person who is entitled to apply for a residence order with respect to a child;

(*d*) an authority, where an order has been made under Article 50(1)(*a*) of the Order of 1995 placing a child in its care;

(*e*) the Official Solicitor if appointed the guardian ad litem of a child of the family under rule 6.6; and

(*f*) a child of the family who has been given leave to intervene in the cause for the purpose of applying for ancillary relief,

28

may apply for an order for ancillary relief as respects that child by notice in Form M13.

(2) In this rule

—"authority" has the meaning assigned to it by Article 2(1) and (3) of the Order of 1995;

—"residence order" has the meaning assigned to it by Article 8(1) of the Order of 1995.

Application in Form M13 or M14

2.57. Where an application for ancillary relief is made by notice in Form M13 or an application under rule 2.48 is made by notice in Form M14, the notice shall—

(*a*) if the cause has been set down for trial in a divorce county court, be filed in the county court office, or

(*b*) in any other case be filed in the Matrimonial Office,

and within 7 days after filing the notice the applicant shall serve a copy on the respondent to the application.

Application for ancillary relief after order of court of summary jurisdiction

2.58. Where an application for ancillary relief is made while there is in force an order of a court of summary jurisdiction for maintenance of a spouse or child, the applicant shall file a copy of the order on or before the hearing of the application.

Children to be separately represented on certain applications

2.59.—(1) Where an application is made to the High Court or a divorce county court for an order for a variation of settlement the court shall, unless it is satisfied that the proposed variation does not adversely affect the rights or interest of any child concerned, direct that the child be separately represented on the application, either by a solicitor or by a solicitor and counsel, and may appoint the Official Solicitor or other fit person to be guardian ad litem of the child for the purpose of the application.

(2) On any other application for ancillary relief the court may give such a direction or make such appointment as it is empowered to give or make by paragraph (1).

(3) Before a person other than the Official Solicitor is appointed guardian ad litem under this rule there shall be filed a certificate by the solicitor acting for the child that the person proposed as guardian has no interest in the matter adverse to that of the child and that he is a proper person to be such guardian.

General provisions as to evidence, etc, on application for ancillary relief

2.60.—(1) A petitioner or respondent who has applied for ancillary relief in his petition or answer and who intends to proceed with the application before the Master shall, subject to rule 2.70, file a notice in Form M15 and within 7 days after doing so serve a copy on the other spouse.

(2) Where a respondent or a petitioner is served with a notice in Form M13 or M15 in respect of an application for ancillary relief, not being an application to which rule 2.58 applies, then, unless the parties are agreed upon the terms of the proposed order, he shall, within 14 days after service of the notice, file an affidavit in answer to the application containing full particulars of his property and income, and if he does not do so, the court may order him to file an affidavit containing such particulars.

(3) Except where the application is for a variation order the applicant shall, within 14 days after service of any affidavit under paragraph (2) or within such other time as the court may fix, file an affidavit in reply containing full particulars of his property and income.

Evidence on application for property adjustment or avoidance of disposition order

2.61.—(1) Where an application is made for a property adjustment order, or an avoidance of disposition order, the application shall state briefly the nature of the adjustment proposed or the disposition to be set aside and the notice in Form M13 or M15, as the case may be, shall, unless the court otherwise directs, be supported by an affidavit by the applicant stating the facts relied on in support of the application.

(2) The affidavit in support shall contain, so far as known to the applicant, full particulars—

(*a*) in the case of an application for a transfer or settlement of property—

(i) of the property in respect of which the application is made,

(ii) of the property to which the party against whom the application is made is entitled in possession or in reversion;

(*b*) in the case of an application for a variation of settlement order—

(i) of all settlements, whether ante-nuptial or post-nuptial, made on the spouses, and

(ii) of the funds brought into settlement by each spouse;

(*c*) in the case of an application for an avoidance of disposition order—

(i) of the property to which the disposition relates,

(ii) of the persons in whose favour the disposition is alleged to have been made and, in the case of a disposition alleged to have been made by way of settlement, of the trustees and the beneficiaries of the settlement.

(3) Where an application for a property adjustment order or an avoidance of disposition order relates to land, the affidavit in support shall, in addition to containing any particulars required by paragraph (2)—

(*a*) state if known to the applicant, whether the title to the land is registered or unregistered and, if registered, the Land Registry folio number,

(*b*) give particulars, so far as known to the applicant, of any mortgage, charge or lien whatsoever on the land or on any interest therein.

(4) A copy of Form M13 or M15, as the case may be, together with a copy of the supporting affidavit, shall be served on the following persons as well as on the respondent to the application, that is to say—

(*a*) in the case of an application for a variation of settlement order, the trustees of the settlement and the settlor if living,

(*b*) in the case of an application for an avoidance of disposition order, the person in whose favour the disposition is alleged to have been made,

(*c*) in the case of an application to which paragraph 3 refers, any mortgagee or chargee or person who claims a lien on the property of whose interest particulars are given pursuant to that paragraph,

and such other persons, if any, as the Master may direct.

(5) Any person served with notice of an application to which this rule applies may, within 14 days after service, file an affidavit in answer.

Evidence on application for variation order

2.62. An application for a variation order shall be supported by an affidavit by the applicant setting out full particulars of his property and income and the grounds on which the application is made.

Service of affidavit in answer or reply

2.63.—(1) a person who files an affidavit for use on an application under rule 2.60, 2.61 or 2.62 shall at the same time serve a copy on the opposite party and, where the affidavit contains an allegation of adultery or of improper conduct with a named person, then, unless the court otherwise directs, it shall be indorsed with a notice in Form M16, and a copy of the affidavit or of such part thereof as the court may direct, indorsed as aforesaid, shall be served on that person by the person who files the affidavit, and the person against whom the allegation is made shall be entitled to intervene in the proceedings by applying for directions under rule 2.64(6) within 7 days after service of the affidavit on him.

(2) Rule 2.35(3) shall apply to a person served with an affidavit under paragraph (1) of this rule as it applies to a co-respondent.

Investigation by Master of application for ancillary relief

2.64.—(1) On or after the filing of a notice in Form M13 or M15 an appointment shall be fixed for the hearing of the application by the Master.

(2) An application for an avoidance of disposition order shall, if practicable, be heard at the same time as any related application for financial relief.

(3) Notice of the appointment, unless given in Form M13 or M15 (as the case may be) shall be given to every party to the application.

(4) Any party to an application for ancillary relief may by letter require any other party to give further information concerning any matter contained in any affidavit filed by or on behalf of that other party or any other relevant matter, or to furnish a list of relevant documents or to allow inspection of any

such document, and may, in default of compliance by such other party, apply to the Master for directions.

(5) At the hearing of an application for ancillary relief the Master shall, subject to rules 2.65 and 2.66, investigate the allegation made in support of and in answer to the application, and may take evidence orally and may at any stage of the proceedings, whether before or during the hearing, order the attendance of any person for the purpose of being examined or cross-examined, and order the discovery and production of any document or require further affidavits.

(6) The Master may at any stage of the proceedings give directions as to the filing and service of pleadings and as to the further conduct of the proceedings.

(7) Where any party to such an application intends on the day appointed for the hearing to apply only for directions, he shall file and serve on every other party a notice to that effect.

Order on application for ancillary relief

2.65.—(1) Subject to rule 2.66, the Master shall, after completing his investigation under rule 2.64, make such order as he thinks just.

(2) Pending the final determination of the application, the Master may make an interim order upon such terms as he thinks just.

Reference of application to judge

2.66. The Master may at any time refer an application for ancillary relief, or any question arising thereon, to the judge for his decision.

Transfer of application for ancillary relief: general provisions

2.67.—(1) If a county court considers that an application for ancillary relief pending in that court gives rise to a contested issue of conduct of a nature which is likely materially to affect the question whether any, or what, order should be made therein and that for that reason the application should be transferred to the High Court, the court shall, subject to paragraph (5), make an order for transfer accordingly and, where an application is transferred to the High Court under this paragraph, it shall be heard by a judge.

(2) Where an application for ancillary relief is pending in a county court and the parties to the proceedings consent to the making of an order for the transfer of the application to the High Court, an application for that purpose may be made to the Master who shall, subject to paragraph (5), either order the transfer or refer the application to the judge for his decision.

(3) Without prejudice to paragraph (1) and (2), the court in which an application for ancillary relief is pending may, if it is a county court, order the transfer of the application to the High Court or, if it is the High Court, order the transfer of the application to a county court, where the transfer appears to the court to be desirable.

(4) The judge before hearing and the Master before investigating under rule 2.64 an application for ancillary relief pending in a county court shall

consider whether the case is one in which the court should exercise any of its powers under paragraph (1) or (3).

(5) In considering whether an application should be transferred from a county court to the High Court or from the High Court to a county court, the court shall have regard to all relevant considerations, including the nature and value of the property involved and the relief sought.

(6) Where a decree nisi has been pronounced in the cause, the court shall, before making an order for the transfer of the application to the High Court, consider whether it would be more convenient to transfer the cause to the High Court under rule 2.32.

(7) Where an application for ancillary relief is pending in a county court, the court may order that the application be transferred to another county court.

(8) An order under paragraph (1), (3) or (7) may be made by the court of its own motion or on the application of a party, but before making an order of its own motion the court shall give the parties an opportunity of being heard, and for that purpose shall cause notice to be given to the parties of the date, time and place at which the question will be considered.

Transfer for purpose of expedition

2.68. Without prejudice to the last foregoing rule, a judge or Master may, on the application of a party or of his own motion, order that an application for ancillary relief pending in the High Court or a divorce county court shall be transferred to a divorce county court or the High Court if he is of opinion that the transfer is desirable for the purpose of expediting the hearing of the application.

Arrangements for hearing of application etc by judge

2.69.—(1) Where an application for ancillary relief or any question arising thereon has been referred or adjourned to the judge, the proper officer or chief clerk, as the case may be, shall fix a date and time for the hearing of the application or the consideration of the question and give notice thereof to all parties.

(2) The hearing or consideration shall, unless the judge otherwise directs, take place in chambers.

(3) Where the application is proceeding in a divorce county court, the hearing or consideration may be transferred to such county court as, in the opinion of the Master, is the most convenient.

Request for periodical payments order at same rate as order for maintenance pending suit

2.70.—(1) Where at or after the date of a decree nisi of divorce or nullity of marriage an order for maintenance pending suit is in force, the party in whose favour the order was made may, if he has made an application for an order for periodical payments for himself in his petition or answer, as the case may be, request the Master in writing to make such an order (in this rule referred to as a "corresponding order") providing for payments at the same rate as those provided for by the order for maintenance pending suit.

33

(2) Where such a request is made, the applicant shall serve on the other spouse a notice in Form M17 requiring him, if he objects to the making of a corresponding order, to give notice to that effect to the proper officer or chief clerk, as the case may be, and to the applicant, within 14 days after service of the notice in Form M17.

(3) If the other spouse does not give notice of objection within the time aforesaid the Master may make a corresponding order without further notice to that spouse and without requiring the attendance of the applicant or his solicitor.

Application for order under Article 39(2)(a) of the Order of 1978

2.71.—(1) An application under Article 39(2)(*a*) of the Order of 1978 for an order restraining any person from attempting to defeat a claim for financial provision or otherwise for protecting the claim may be made to the Master.

(2) Rules 2.66 and 2.69 shall apply, with the necessary modifications, to the application as if it were an application for ancillary relief.

Consent orders

2.72.—(1) Subject to paragraphs (2) and (3), there shall be lodged with every application for a consent order under any of Articles 25, 26 or 29 of the Order of 1978, a draft of the order in the terms sought, endorsed with a statement signed by the respondent to the application signifying his agreement, and a statement of information which may be made in more than one document and shall include:

(*a*) particulars of the duration of the marriage, the age of each party and of any minor or dependant child of the family;

(*b*) an estimate in summary form of the approximate amount or value of the capital resources and net income of each party and of any minor child of the family;

(*c*) what arrangements are intended for the accommodation of each of the parties and any minor child of the family;

(*d*) whether either party has remarried or has any present intention to marry or to cohabit with another person;

(*e*) where the terms of the order provide for a transfer of property, a statement confirming that any mortgagee of that property has been served with notice of the application and that no objection to such a transfer has been made by the mortgagee within 14 days from such service; and

(*f*) any other especially significant matters.

(2) Where an application is made for a consent order varying an order for periodical payments, paragraph (1) shall be sufficiently complied with if the statement of information required to be lodged with the application includes only the information in respect of net income mentioned in paragraph (1)(*b*), and an application for a consent order for interim periodical payments

pending the determination of an application for ancillary relief may be made in like manner.

(3) Where the parties attend the hearing of an application for financial relief the court may dispense with the filing of a draft of the order and a statement of information in accordance with paragraph (1) and give directions for:

(a) the order to be drawn; and

(b) the information which would otherwise be required to be given, in such manner as it sees fit.

Pensions

2.73.—(1) Where an applicant for ancillary relief or the respondent to the application is obliged by rule 2.60 to give full particulars of his property and income, he shall also give full particulars of any benefits under a pension scheme which he has or is likely to have including the most recent valuation (if any) of the benefits under the scheme.

(2) Where by virtue of rule 2.64(5) the Master has power to order discovery of any document he shall also have power to require either party to request a valuation of benefits which he has or is likely to have under any pension scheme from the trustees or managers of the scheme.

(3) A petitioner or respondent who has applied for ancillary relief, not including provision made by Article 27B or 27C of the Order of 1978 may at any time amend the application so as to include such provision by way of a notice or amended notice in Form M13 and rule 2.57 shall apply to any such notice.

(4) A petitioner or respondent who has applied for an order which by virtue of Article 27B or 27C of the Order of 1978 imposes any requirement on the trustees or managers of a pension scheme shall, within 4 days after filing the notice in Form M13 or M15 as the case may be, serve on those trustees or managers a copy of that notice, together with the following—

(a) an address to which any notice the trustees or managers may be required to serve is to be sent;

(b) an address to which any payment which the trustees or managers are required to make to the applicant is to be sent; and

(c) where the address in sub-paragraph (b) is that of a bank, a building society or the Department of National Savings sufficient details to enable payment to be made into the account of the applicant.

(5) Where the petitioner and the respondent have agreed on the terms of an order which by virtue of Article 27B or 27C of the Order of 1978 imposes any requirement on the trustees or managers of a pension scheme they shall with 4 days after notifying the court of their agreement serve on the trustees or managers a copy of the agreed terms together with the particulars set out in paragraph (4)(a), (b) and (c).

(6) Trustees or managers of a pension scheme on whom a copy of such a notice is served may, within 14 days after service, require the applicant to provide them with a copy of the affidavit supporting his application.

(7) Trustees or managers of a pension scheme who receive a copy of an affidavit as required pursuant to paragraph (5) may within 14 days after receipt file an affidavit in answer.

(8) Trustees or managers of a pension scheme who file an affidavit pursuant to paragraph (6) may file therewith a notice requiring an appointment to be fixed; and where such a notice is filed—

> (a) the proper officer or chief clerk shall fix an appointment for the hearing or further hearing of the application and shall give not less than 14 days' notice of that appointment to the petitioner, the respondent and the trustees or managers of the pension scheme; and

> (b) the trustees or managers of the pension scheme shall be entitled to be represented at any such hearing.

(9) In deciding whether to make an order which by virtue of Article 27B or 27C of the Order of 1978 imposes any requirement on the trustees or managers of a pension scheme, the court shall take into account any representations of the trustees or managers as to whether, in all the circumstances of the case, the court ought to make the order, and in particular whether the particulars supplied under paragraph (4) are sufficient to enable the trustees or managers to comply with their obligations under any such order.

(10) Expressions used in this rule have the same meaning as in Article 27D of the Order of 1978.

PART III

OTHER FAMILY PROCEEDINGS

Application by spouse for failure to maintain

3.1.—(1) An application under Article 29 of the Order of 1978 by a party to a marriage who alleges that the other party to the marriage—

> (a) has failed to provide reasonable maintenance for the applicant, or

> (b) has failed to provide, or to make a proper contribution towards, reasonable maintenance for any child of the family,

shall be made by originating summons in Form M18. Such summons shall be issued out of—

> (i) the Matrimonial Office in relation to applications to the High Court;

> (ii) a county court office, in relation to applications to a county court.

(2) There shall be filed in support of the summons an affidavit by the applicant which shall state—

> (a) the names of the parties to the marriage, the place and date of the marriage;

> (b) the names of each child and his date of birth, or if it be the case that he is over 18 years of age, and in the case of each minor child over the age of 16 years whether he is, or will be, or if an order for provision

36

were made would be, receiving instruction at an educational establishment or undergoing training for a trade, profession or vocation and the person with whom any such child is residing;

(c) if there have been any previous proceedings in any court in Northern Ireland or elsewhere with reference to the marriage or children of the marriage or between the applicant and respondent with reference to any property of either or both of them, the date and effect of any decree or order, and in the case of proceedings in reference to the marriage if there has been any resumption of cohabitation since the making of the decree or order;

(d) where the application is for periodical payments or secured periodical payments for a child—

(i) whether the application is

— for a stepchild;

— in addition to child support maintenance already payable under a Child Support Agency assessment;

— to meet expenses arising from a child's disability;

— to meet expenses incurred by a child being educated or trained for work; or

— made on some other specified ground;

(ii) if the child or the person with care of the child or the absent parent of the child is not habitually resident in the United Kingdom;

(e) particulars of the alleged failure to maintain;

(f) whether there are or have been any proceedings in the Child Support Agency with reference to the maintenance of each child and if so the details of those proceedings;

(g) the means of the applicant and the respondent;

(h) the facts upon which it is claimed that the court has jurisdiction to entertain the proceedings.

(3) If the proper officer or chief clerk, as the case may be, does not consider it practicable to fix a day for the hearing of the application at the time when it is issued he may do so subsequently and in that case he shall forthwith give notice of the day to all parties.

(4) Within 21 days after the time limited for giving notice of intention to defend, the respondent shall, if he intends to contest the application, file an affidavit in answer setting out the grounds on which he relies (including any allegation which he wishes to make against the applicant), and shall in any case, unless the court otherwise directs, file an affidavit containing full particulars of his property and income and serve a copy of the affidavit on the applicant.

(5) Where the respondent's affidavit alleges adultery the alleged adulterer shall, unless the court otherwise directs, be made a party cited and be served with a copy of the affidavit, with notice in Form M19, and rule 2.8 shall apply, with the necessary modifications, as if the affidavit were a petition and the party cited were a co-respondent.

(6) A party cited who wishes to defend all or any of the charges made against him shall within 21 days after the time limited for giving notice of intention to defend, file an affidavit in answer and serve a copy of the affidavit on the respondent.

(7) If the respondent does not file an affidavit in accordance with paragraph (4), the court may order him to file an affidavit containing full particulars of his property and income and serve a copy of any such affidavit on the applicant.

(8) Within 14 days after being served with a copy of any affidavit in answer filed by the respondent the applicant may file an affidavit in reply and serve a copy on the respondent and on any party cited. No further affidavit shall be filed without leave.

Transfer to High Court of applications under rule 3.1

3.2.—(1) Where it appears to a divorce county court that the respondent intends to contest an application under the last foregoing rule on the ground that—

(*a*) by reason of the applicant's conduct or otherwise the respondent is not liable to maintain the applicant, or

(*b*) no court in Northern Ireland has jurisdiction to entertain the application,

the court shall order that the application be transferred to the High Court.

Hearing of applications under rule 3.1

3.3.—(1) Without prejudice to the provisions of rule 3.2, rules 2.67 (except paragraphs (5) and (7) thereof) and 2.68 shall apply with the necessary modifications to an application for an order under Article 29 of the Order of 1978 as if the application were an application for ancillary relief.

(2) The application shall be heard by a judge in chambers, and, if the application is to a divorce county court, the hearing shall be fixed to take place at such court as in the opinion of the chief clerk is the most convenient.

(3) On the hearing of the application the judge may make such order as he thinks just or may refer the application (except any application under Article 8 of the Order of 1995), or any application for an order under Article 29(5) of the Order of 1978 to the Master for him to investigate the means of the parties to the marriage.

(4) Where an application is referred to the Master under paragraph (3), the proper officer or the chief clerk, as the case may be, shall fix an appointment for the hearing of the application and thereupon the provisions of these Rules relating to ancillary relief shall apply except that where the judge has not made a finding that there has been wilful neglect to maintain—

(*a*) the Master shall, after completing his investigation under rule 2.64, report the result thereof in writing to a judge to whom the application shall be adjourned;

(*b*) the Master's report shall contain an estimate of the financial relief to which, in his opinion, the applicant would be entitled if the application were granted;

(*c*) the Master's report shall be filed and any party shall be entitled to inspect the report and to be supplied with a copy of it on payment of the prescribed fee.

(5) Where a person has been made a party cited, the judge may, if after the close of the evidence on the part of the respondent he is of opinion that there is not sufficient evidence against the party cited, dismiss him from the proceedings.

(6) Subject to the provisions of this rule and of rules 3.1 and 3.2, these Rules shall, so far as applicable, apply with the necessary modifications to an application under Article 29 of the Order of 1978 as if—

(*a*) the application were a cause, and

(*b*) the originating summons were a petition and the applicant the petitioner.

Application for alteration of maintenance agreement during lifetime of parties

3.4.—(1) An application to the court under Article 37 of the Order of 1978 for the alteration of a maintenance agreement during the lifetime of the parties shall be made by originating summons in accordance with Form M20.

(2) The application may be filed in the Matrimonial Office or a county court office and may be heard and determined by the Master.

(3) There shall be filed in support of the summons an affidavit by the applicant exhibiting a copy of the agreement and stating—

(*a*) the residence of the parties to the agreement at the date of the application and, unless both parties are then resident in Northern Ireland, their domicile at that date;

(*b*) the date and place of the marriage between the parties to the agreement and the name and status of the wife before the marriage;

(*c*) the full names (including surnames) of any children of the family and of any other children for whom the agreement makes financial arrangements and—

    (i) the date of birth of each child, now living or, if it be the case, that he is over 18 years of age, and, in the case of each minor over 16 years of age, whether he is or will be, or if an order or provision were made would be, receiving instruction at an educational establishment or undergoing training for a trade, profession or vocation and the place where and the person with whom any minor child is residing;

    (ii) the date of death of any such child who has died since the agreement was made;

(*d*) whether there have been any previous proceedings in any court with reference to the agreement or to the marriage or to any child of the family or of the other children for whom the agreement makes financial arrangements or between the applicant and respondent with reference to any property of either or both of them, and the date and effect of any order made;

39

(*e*) whether there are or have been any proceedings in the Child Support Agency with reference to the maintenance of each child and if so the details of those proceedings;

(*f*) the means of the applicant and the other party to the agreement insofar as they are within the applicant's knowledge or belief;

(*g*) the nature of the alteration of the agreement sought and the facts alleged by the applicant to justify the alterations.

(4) A copy of the affidavit shall be served on the respondent with the summons.

(5) The respondent shall, within 14 days after the time limited for giving notice of intention to defend, file an affidavit in answer to the application containing full particulars of his property and income and, if he does not do so, the court may order him to file an affidavit containing such particulars.

(6) A respondent who files an affidavit under paragraph (5) shall serve a copy on the applicant.

Application for alteration of maintenance agreement after death of one party

3.5.—(1) An application under Article 38 of the Order of 1978 for the alteration of a maintenance agreement after the death of one of the parties to it shall be made by originating summons in Form M21.

(2) The application may be filed in the Matrimonial Office or a county court office and may be heard and determined by the Master.

(3) There shall be filed in support of the summons an affidavit by the applicant exhibiting a copy of the agreement and an office copy of the grant of representation to the deceased's estate and of every testamentary document admitted to proof.

(4) The affidavit referred to in paragraph (2) shall state—

(*a*) whether the deceased died domiciled in Northern Ireland;

(*b*) the place and date of the marriage between the parties to the agreement and the name and status of the wife before the marriage;

(*c*) the name of every child of the family and of any other child for whom the agreement makes financial arrangements, and—

(i) the date of birth of each such child who is still living (or, if it be the case, that he has attained 18 years), and the place where the person with whom any such minor child is residing;

(ii) the date of death of any such child who has died since the agreement was made;

(*d*) whether there have been in any court any, and if so what, previous proceedings with reference to the agreement or to the marriage or to the children of the family or to any other children for whom the agreement makes financial arrangements, and the date and effect of any order or decree made in such proceedings;

(*e*) whether there have been in any court any proceedings by the applicant against the deceased's estate under the Inheritance (Provision for

Family and Dependants) (Northern Ireland) Order 1979(**a**) or any statutory provision repealed by that Order and the date and effect of any order made in such proceedings;

(*f*) in the case of an application by the surviving party, the applicant's means;

(*g*) in the case of an application by the personal representatives of the deceased, the surviving party's means, so far as they are known to the applicants, and the information mentioned in sub-paragraph (*a*), (*b*) and (*c*) of rule 3.6(2);

(*h*) the facts alleged by the applicant as justifying an alteration in the agreement and the nature of the alteration sought;

(*i*) if the application is made after the end of the period of six months from the date on which representation in regard to the deceased's estate was first taken out, the grounds on which the court's permission to entertain the application is sought.

Further proceedings on an application under rule 3.5

3.6.—(1) The court may at any stage of the proceedings direct that any person be added as a respondent to an application under rule 3.5.

(2) A respondent who is a personal representative of the deceased shall, within 14 days after the time limited for entered an appearance, file an affidavit in answer to the application stating—

(*a*) full particulars of the value of the deceased's estate for probate, after providing for the discharge of the funeral, testamentary and administration expenses, debts and liabilities payable thereout, including the amount of the capital transfer tax and interest thereon;

(*b*) the person or classes of person beneficially interested in the estate (giving the names and addresses of all living beneficiaries) and the value of their interests so far as ascertained; and

(*c*) if such be the case, that any living beneficiary (naming him) is a minor or a patient.

(3) If a respondent who is a personal representative of the deceased does not file an affidavit stating the matters mentioned in paragraph (3), the court may order him to do so.

(4) A respondent who is not a personal representative of the deceased may, within 14 days after the time limited for entering an appearance, file an affidavit in answer to the application.

Application of other rules to proceedings under Article 37 or 38 of the Order of 1978

3.7.—(1) Rules 2.63; 2.64(1) and (4) to (7), 2.65, 2.66 and 2.69 shall apply, with the necessary modifications, to an application under Article 37 or 38 of the Order of 1978 as if it were an application for ancillary relief.

(**a**) S.I. 1979/924 (N.I. 8)

(2) Subject to paragraph (1) and to the provisions of rule 3.4, these Rules shall, so far as applicable, apply with the necessary modifications to an application under Article 37 or 38 of the Order of 1978 as if the application were a cause, the originating summons a petition, and the applicant the petitioner.

Proceedings in respect of polygamous marriage

3.8.—(1) The provisions of this rule shall have effect where a petition or originating summons asks for matrimonial relief within the meaning of Article 50(2) of the Order of 1978 in respect of a marriage entered into under a law which permits polygamy (in this rule referred to as a polygamous marriage).

(2) The petition or originating summons—

(*a*) shall state that the marriage in question is polygamous;

(*b*) in respect of the additional spouse, shall give his or her full name and address and the date and place of his or her marriage to the petitioner or applicant or, as the case may be, to the respondent or state, so far as may be applicable, that such information is unknown to the petitioner or applicant.

(3) In this rule "additional spouse" means any living spouse of the petitioner or applicant additional to the respondent or as the case may be any living spouse of the respondent additional to the petitioner or applicant.

(4) Without prejudice to its powers under R.S.C. Order 15 (which deals with causes of action, counterclaims and parties) or C.C.R. Order 9 (which deals with amendments), the court may order that any additional spouse be added as a party to the proceedings or be given notice of the proceedings or of any application in the proceedings for any such order as is mentioned in Article 50(2)(*d*) of the Order of 1978.

(5) Any order under paragraph (4) may be made at any stage of the proceedings and either on the application of any party or by the court of its own motion and, where an additional spouse is mentioned in a petition or an acknowledgement of service of a petition, the petitioner shall, on making any application in the proceedings or, if no previous application has been made in the proceedings, on lodging the certificate of readiness, ask for directions as to whether an order should be made under paragraph (3).

(6) Any person to whom notice is given pursuant to an order under paragraph (4) shall be entitled, without filing an answer or affidavit, to be heard in the proceedings or on the application to which the notice relates.

Transfer of certain tenancies on divorce

3.9.—(1) The jurisdiction of the court under Article 41 of, and Schedule 1 to, the Order of 1989 may be exercised by the Master.

(2) Where an application is made for an order under Part II of the said Schedule 1 notice of the application shall be served by the applicant on—

(*a*) the spouse entitled to occupy the dwelling house to which the application relates; and (*b*) the landlord of the dwelling house,

and any person so served shall be entitled to be heard on the application.

(3) Where the court intends to make an order under the said Schedule 1 then, before making the order, the court shall cause notice of its intention to make the order to be given to the landlord and shall afford him an opportunity of being heard.

Application for declaration as to marital status

3.10.—(1) Unless otherwise directed, a petition by which proceedings are begun under Article 31 of the Order of 1989 for a declaration as to marital status shall state—

(*a*) the names of the parties to the marriage to which the application relates and the residential address of each of them at the date of the presentation of the petition;

(*b*) the place and date of any ceremony of marriage to which the application relates;

(*c*) the grounds on which the application is made and all other material facts alleged by the petitioner to justify the making of the declaration;

(*d*) whether there have been or are continuing any proceedings in any court, tribunal or authority in Northern Ireland or elsewhere between the parties which relate to, or are capable of affecting the validity or subsistence of the marriage, divorce, annulment or legal separation to which the application relates, or which relate to the matrimonial status of either of the parties, and if so—

(i) the nature, and either the outcome or present state of those proceedings,

(ii) the court, tribunal or authority before which they were begun,

(iii) the date when they were begun,

(iv) the names of the parties to them,

(v) the date or expected date of the trial,

(vi) any other facts relevant to the question whether the petition should be stayed under Schedule 1 of the Order,

and such proceedings shall include any which are constituted otherwise than in a court of law in any country outside Northern Ireland, if they are instituted before a tribunal or other authority having power under the law having effect there to determine questions of status, and shall be treated as continuing if they have begun and have not been finally disposed of;

(*e*) where it is alleged that the court has jurisdiction based on domicile, which of the parties to the marriage to which the application relates is domiciled in Northern Ireland on the date of the presentation of the petition, or died before that date and was at death domiciled in Northern Ireland;

(*f*) where it is alleged that the court has jurisdiction based on habitual residence, which of the parties to the marriage to which the application

43

relates has been habitually resident in Northern Ireland, on the date of the presentation of the petition, or died before that date and had been habitually resident in Northern Ireland throughout the period of one year ending with the date of death;

(g) where the petitioner was not a party to the marriage to which the application relates, particulars of his interest in the determination of the application.

(2) Where the proceedings are for a declaration that the validity of a divorce, annulment or legal separation obtained in any country outside Northern Ireland in respect of the marriage either is or is not entitled to recognition in Northern Ireland, the petition shall in addition state the date and place of the divorce, annulment or legal separation.

(3) There shall be annexed to the petition a copy of the certificate of any marriage to which the application relates, or, as the case may be, a certified copy of any decree of divorce, annulment or order for legal separation to which the application relates.

(4) Where a document produced by virtue of paragraph (3) is not in English it shall, unless the court otherwise directs, be accompanied by a translation certified by a notary public or authenticated by affidavit.

(5) The parties to the marriage in respect of which a declaration is sought shall be petitioner and respondent respectively to the application, unless a third party is applying for a declaration, in which case he shall be the petitioner and the parties shall be respondents to the application.

Procedure to be followed in relation to application under rule 3.10

3.11.—(1) The petition referred to in rule 3.10 shall be supported by an affidavit by the petitioner verifying the petition and giving particulars of every person whose interest may be affected by the proceedings and his relationship to the petitioner:

Provided that if the petitioner is under the age of 18, the affidavit shall, unless the court otherwise directs, be made by his next friend.

(2) Where the jurisdiction of the court to entertain a petition is based on habitual residence the petition shall include a statement of the addresses of the places of residence of the person so resident and the length of residence at each place either during the period of one year ending with the date of the presentation of the petition or, if that person is dead, throughout the period of one year ending with the date of death.

(3) An affidavit for the purposes of paragraph (1) may contain statements of information or belief with the sources and grounds thereof.

(4) A copy of the petition and every document accompanying it shall be sent by the petitioner to the Crown Solicitor on behalf of the Attorney General at least one month before the petition is filed and it shall not be necessary thereafter to serve these documents upon him.

(5) The proper officer or chief clerk, as the case may be, shall send a copy of any answer to the Crown Solicitor on behalf of the Attorney General

if he has notified the proper officer or chief clerk that he wishes to intervene in the proceedings.

(6) When all answers to the petition have been filed the petitioner shall lodge in the Matrimonial Office and serve on all respondents to the application a request for directions as to any other persons who should be made respondents to the petition or given notice of the proceedings.

(7) When giving directions in accordance with paragraph (6) the court shall consider whether it is necessary that the Attorney General should argue before it any question relating to the proceedings, and if it does so consider, the Attorney General need not file an answer and the court shall give directions requiring him to serve on all parties to the proceedings a summary of his argument.

(8) Persons given notice of the proceedings pursuant to directions given in accordance with paragraph (6) shall within 21 days after service of the notice upon them be entitled to apply to the Master to be joined as parties.

(9) The Attorney General may file an answer to the petition within 21 days after directions have been given under paragraph (7) and notice of hearing shall not be given until that period and the period referred to in paragraph (8) have expired.

(10) The Attorney General in deciding whether it is necessary or expedient to intervene in the proceedings, may have a search made for, and may inspect and bespeak a copy of, any document filed in the court which relates to any other matrimonial proceedings referred to in the proceedings.

(11) A declaration made in accordance with Article 31 of the Order of 1989 shall be in Form M26.

Application for leave to apply for financial relief after overseas divorce

3.12.—(1) An application to the High Court for leave to apply for an order for financial relief under Part IV of the Order of 1989 shall be made ex parte by originating summons in Form M27 issued out of the Matrimonial Office and shall be supported by an affidavit by the applicant stating the facts relied on in support of the application with particular reference to the matters set out in Article 20(2) of that Order.

(2) The affidavit in support shall give particulars of the judicial or other proceedings by means of which the marriage to which the application relates was dissolved or annulled or by which the parties to the marriage were legally separated and shall state, so far as is known to the applicant:—

(a) the names of the parties to the marriage and the date and place of the marriage;

(b) the occupation and residence of each of the parties to the marriage;

(c) whether there are any living children of the family and, if so, the number of such children and full names (including surname) of each and his date of birth or, if it be the case, that he is over 18;

(d) whether either party to the marriage has remarried;

(*e*) an estimate in summary form of the approximate amount or value of the capital resources and net income of each party and of any minor child of the family;

(*f*) the grounds on which it is alleged that the court has jurisdiction to entertain an application for financial relief under Part IV of the Order of 1989.

(3) The proper officer shall fix a date and time for the hearing of the application by the judge in chambers and give notice thereof to the applicant.

Application for an order for financial relief or an avoidance of transaction order under Part IV of the Order of 1989

3.13.—(1) An application to the High Court for an order for financial relief under Part IV of the Order of 1989 shall be made by originating summons in Form M28 issued out of the Matrimonial Office and at the same time the applicant, unless otherwise directed, shall file an affidavit in support of the summons giving full particulars of his property and income.

(2) The applicant shall serve a sealed copy of the originating summons on the respondent and shall annex thereto a copy of the affidavit in support, if one has been filed, and a notice of proceedings and acknowledgement of service in Form M30, and rule 2.10 shall apply to such an acknowledgement of service as if the references in paragraph (1) of that rule to Form M6 and in paragraph (2) to 14 days were, respectively, references to Form M30 and 31 days.

(3) Rules 2.59, 2.61, 2.62, 2.64(4), (6) and (7), 2.72(1) and (2) shall apply, with the necessary modifications, to an application for an order for financial relief under this rule as they apply to an application for ancillary relief made by notice in Form M13 and the court may order the attendance of any person for the purpose of being examined or cross-examined and the discovery and production of any document.

(4) An application for an interim order for maintenance under Article 18 of the Order of 1989 or an avoidance of transaction order under Article 27 of that Order may be made, unless the court otherwise directs, in the originating summons under paragraph (1) or by summons in accordance with rule 7.5 and an application for an order under the said Article 27 shall be supported by an affidavit, which may be the affidavit filed under paragraph (1), stating the facts relied on.

(5) If the respondent intends to contest the application he shall, within 28 days after the time limited for giving notice to defend, file an affidavit in answer to the application setting out the grounds on which he relies and shall serve a copy on the applicant.

(6) In respect of any application for an avoidance of transaction order the court may make such order as it is empowered to make by paragraph (3) and rule 2.61 shall apply, with the necessary modifications, to an application for an avoidance of transaction order as it applies to an avoidance of disposition order.

(7) Where the originating summons contains an application for an order under Article 26 of the Order of 1989 the applicant shall serve a copy on the

landlord of the dwelling-house and he shall be entitled to be heard on the application.

(8) Where, in reliance on Article 26 of the Order of 1989, the court intends to make an order under Part II of Schedule 1 to that Order then, before making the order, the court shall cause notice of its intention to make the order to be given to the landlord of the dwelling-house and shall afford him an opportunity of being heard.

(9) An application for an order for financial relief under Part IV of the Order of 1989 or for an avoidance of transaction order shall be determined by the judge.

Application for an order under Article 28 of the Order of 1989 preventing a transaction

3.14.—(1) An application to the High Court under Article 28 of the Order of 1989 for an order preventing a transaction shall be made by originating summons in Form M29 issued out of the Matrimonial Office and shall be supported by an affidavit by the applicant stating the facts relied on in support of the application.

(2) The applicant shall serve a sealed copy of the originating summons on the respondent and shall annex thereto a copy of the affidavit in support and a notice of proceedings and acknowledgement of service in Form M30, and rule 2.11 shall apply to such an acknowledgement of service as if the references in paragraph (1) of that rule to Form M6 and in paragraph (2) of that rule to 14 days were, respectively, references to Form M30 and 31 days.

(3) If the respondent intends to contest the application he shall within 28 days after the time limited for giving notice to defend, file an affidavit in answer to the application setting out the grounds on which he relies and shall serve a copy on the applicant.

(4) The application shall be determined by the judge.

(5) Rule 2.68 (except paragraph (3)) shall apply, with the necessary modifications, to the applications as if it were an application for ancillary relief.

PART IV

CHILDREN (NORTHERN IRELAND) ORDER 1995

Interpretation and application

4.1.—(1) In this Part of and in Appendix 3 to these Rules, unless a contrary intention appears—

"the Allocation Order" means the Children (Allocation of Proceedings) Order (Northern Ireland) 1996(**a**);

an Article or Schedule referred to by number means the Article or Schedule so numbered in the Order of 1995;

(**a**) S.R. 1996 No. 300

"an Article 8 order" has the same meaning as in Article 8(2);

"application" means an application made under or by virtue of the Order of 1995 or under these Rules and "applicant" shall be construed accordingly;

"authority" has the same meaning as in Article 2(2);

"child", in relation to proceedings to which this Part applies—

(a) means, subject to sub-paragraph (b), a person under the age of 18 with respect to whom the proceedings are brought, and

(b) where the proceedings are under Schedule 1, also includes a person who has reached the age of 18;

"directions appointment" means a hearing for directions under rule 4.15;

"family care centre" means a county court which has been specified as a family care centre in the Allocation Order;

"guardian ad litem" means a guardian ad litem, appointed under Article 60, of the child with respect to whom the proceedings are brought;

"leave" includes permission and approval;

"parental responsibility" has the same meaning as in Article 6;

"Parties" means the respondents specified in column (iii) of Appendix 3 and the applicant;

"specified proceedings" has the same meaning as in Article 60(6) and Rule 4.3(2);

"welfare officer" means a person who has been asked to prepare a welfare report under Article 4.

(2) Except where the contrary intention appears, the provisions of this Part apply to proceedings in the High Court and a county court—

(a) on an application for an Article 8 order;

(b) on an application for a care order or supervision order under Article 50;

(c) on an application under Articles 7(1)(a), 7(4), 13(1), 16(6), 33, 44, 52(7), 53(2), 53(3), 53(4), 53(9), 55(1), 57(8)(b), 58(1), 58(2), 58(3), 58(4), 62(1), 62(12), 63, 64, 67(9), 69(1), 159(1), 163(1), 178(1);

(d) under Schedule 1, except, where financial relief is also sought by or on behalf of an adult;

(e) on an application under paragraph 6(3) of Schedule 3;

(f) on an application under paragraph 5(2) or 7(1) of Schedule 4; or

(g) on an application under paragraph 10(3) or 12(4) of Schedule 8.

Proceedings in chambers

4.2. Unless the court otherwise directs proceedings to which this Part applies shall be heard by a judge in chambers.

Matters prescribed for the purposes of the Order of 1995

4.3.—(1) The parties to proceedings in which directions are given under Article 57(6) and any person named in such a direction, form the prescribed class for the purposes of Article 57(8)(*b*) (application to vary directions made with interim care or interim supervision order).

(2) The following proceedings are specified for the purposes of Article 60 in accordance with paragraph 6(*i*) thereof—

(*a*) proceedings under Article 33(1);

(*b*) proceedings under Article 44;

(*c*) applications under Article 52(7);

(*d*) proceedings under paragraph 6(3) of Schedule 3;

(*e*) appeals against the determination of proceedings of a kind set out in sub-paragraphs (*a*) to (*d*).

(3) The applicant for an order that has been made under Article 62(1) and the persons referred to in Article 62(11) may, in any circumstances, apply under Article 62(12) for a child assessment order to be varied or discharged.

(4) The following persons form the prescribed class for the purposes of Article 63(9)(*b*) (application to vary directions)—

(*a*) the parties to the application in which it is sought to vary the directions;

(*b*) the guardian ad litem;

(*c*) the Board or Trust in whose area the child is ordinarily resident;

(*d*) any person who is named in the directions.

Application for leave to commence proceedings

4.4.—(1) Where the leave of the court is required to bring any proceedings to which this Part applies, the person seeking leave shall file—

(*a*) a written request for leave in Form C2 setting out the reasons for the application; and

(*b*) a draft of the application (being the documents referred to in rule 4.5(2)) for the making of which leave is sought together with sufficient copies for one to be served on each respondent.

(2) The documents referred to in paragraph (1) shall—

(*a*) in relation to an application to the High Court be filed in the Office of Care and Protection or, where rule 2.38 applies, in the Matrimonial Office;

(*b*) in relation to an application to a county court be filed in the county court office.

(3) On considering a request for leave filed under paragraph (1), the court shall—

(*a*) grant the request, whereupon the proper officer or chief clerk shall inform the person making the request of the decision, or

(*b*) direct that a date be fixed for the hearing of the request, whereupon the proper officer or chief clerk shall fix such a date and give such notice as the court directs to the person making the request and to such other persons as the court requires to be notified of the date so fixed.

(4) Where leave is granted to bring proceedings to which this Part applies the application shall proceed in accordance with rule 4.5 but paragraph (1)(*a*) of that rule shall not apply.

(5) In the case of a request for leave to bring proceedings under Schedule 1, the draft application under paragraph (1) shall be accompanied by a statement in Form C7A setting out the financial details which the person seeking leave believes to be relevant to the request and containing a declaration that it is true to the maker's best knowledge and belief, together with sufficient copies for one to be served on each respondent.

Application

4.5.—(1) Subject to paragraph (5), an applicant shall—

(*a*) file the documents referred to in paragraph (2) (which documents shall together be called "the application") together with sufficient copies for one to be served on each respondent—

    (i) in relation to an application to the High Court, in the Office of Care and Protection or, where rule 2.38 applies, in the Matrimonial Office;

    (ii) in relation to an application to a county court in the county court office; and

(*b*) serve a copy of the application together with Form C3 and such (if any) of Forms C4 and C7A as are given to him under paragraph (3)(*b*) on each respondent such number of days prior to the date fixed under paragraph 3(*a*) as is specified for that application in column (ii) of Appendix 3.

(2) The documents to be filed under paragraph (1)(*a*) are—

(*a*)   (i) whichever is appropriate of Forms C1 or C2 and

    (ii) such of the supplemental Forms C10 or C11 to C17 as may be appropriate, or

(*b*) where there is no appropriate form a statement in writing of the order sought,

and where the application is made in respect of more than one child, all the children shall be included in one application.

(3) On receipt of the documents filed under paragraph (1)(*a*) the proper officer or chief clerk shall—

(*a*) fix the date for a hearing or a directions appointment allowing sufficient time for the applicant to comply with paragraph (1)(*b*),

(*b*) endorse the date so fixed upon Form C3 and, where appropriate, Form C3A and

(*c*) return forthwith to the applicant the copies of the application and Form C7A if filed with it, together with Form C3 and such of Forms C3A and C4 as are appropriate.

(4) The applicant shall, at the same time as complying with paragraph (1)(*b*) serve Form C3A on the persons set out for the relevant class of proceedings in column (iv) of Appendix 3.

(5) In the case of proceedings under Schedule 1, the application under paragraph (1) shall be accompanied by a statement in Form C7A setting out

50

the financial details which the applicant believes to be relevant to the application and containing a declaration that it is true to the maker's best knowledge and belief, together with sufficient copies for one to be served on each respondent.

Withdrawal of application

4.6.—(1) An application may be withdrawn only with leave of the court.

(2) Subject to paragraph (3), a person seeking leave to withdraw an application shall file and serve on the parties a written request for leave in Form C2 setting out the reasons for the request.

(3) The request under paragraph (2) may be made orally to the court if the parties and, if appointed, either the guardian ad litem or the welfare officer are present.

(4) Upon receipt of a written request under paragraph (2) the court shall—

(*a*) if—

    (i) the parties consent in writing,

    (ii) the guardian ad litem has had an opportunity to make representations, and

    (iii) the court thinks fit,

    grant the request, in which case the proper officer or chief clerk shall notify the parties, any guardian ad litem and any welfare officer of the granting of the request, or

(*b*) direct that a date be fixed for the hearing of the request in which case the proper officer or chief clerk shall give at least 7 days' notice to the parties, the guardian ad litem and the welfare officer, of the date fixed.

Transfer of proceedings

4.7.—(1) Where an application is made, in accordance with Article 9 of the Allocation Order, for an order transferring proceedings from a family proceedings court or other court of summary jurisdiction following the refusal of that court to order such a transfer, the applicant shall—

(*a*) file the application in Form C2 with the chief clerk in the family care centre to which the proceedings are sought to be transferred, together with a copy of the certificate issued by the family proceedings court or other court of summary jurisdiction; and

(*b*) serve a copy of the documents mentioned in sub-paragraph (*a*) personally on all parties to the proceedings which it is sought to have transferred,

within 2 days after receipt by the applicant of the certificate.

(2) Within 2 days after receipt of the documents served under paragraph (1)(*b*) any party other than the applicant may file written representations.

(3) The court shall, not before the fourth day after the filing of the application under paragraph (1) unless the parties consent to earlier consideration, consider the application and either—

(*a*) grant the application whereupon the chief clerk shall inform the parties of that decision, or

(*b*) direct that a date be fixed for the hearing of the application, whereupon the chief clerk shall fix such a date and give not less than 1 day's notice to the parties of the date so fixed.

(4) A copy of an order transferring proceedings to a family care centre in accordance with Article 9 of the Allocation Order, shall be sent by the chief clerk to the court from which the proceedings are transferred.

(5) Where proceedings are transferred to a family care centre in accordance with Article 5 or 8 of the Allocation Order the family care centre shall consider whether to transfer those proceedings to the High Court in accordance with Article 10 of that Order and either—

(*a*) determine that an order for such transfer need not be made;

(*b*) make such an order for transfer;

(*c*) order that a date be fixed for the hearing of the question whether such an order for transfer should be made, whereupon the chief clerk shall give such notice to the parties as the court directs of the date so fixed, or

(*d*) invite the parties to make written representations within a specified period, as to whether such an order should be made; and upon receipt of the representations the court shall act in accordance with sub-paragraphs (*a*), (*b*) or (*c*).

(6) Where proceedings are transferred to the High Court under paragraph (5) any relevant documentation shall be sent by the chief clerk to the Office of Care and Protection.

(7) The proper officer shall notify the parties of an order transferring proceedings from the High Court in accordance with Article 13 or 14 of the Allocation Order and a copy of the order shall be sent to the court to which the proceedings are transferred.

(8) The chief clerk shall notify the parties of an order transferring proceedings in accordance with Article 11 or 12 of the Allocation Order and a copy of the order shall be sent to the court to which the proceedings are transferred.

(9) An order under this rule transferring proceedings in accordance with the Allocation Order shall be in Form C43 and shall be served on the parties by the proper officer or chief clerk as the case may be.

Parties

4.8.—(1) The respondents to proceedings to which this Part applies shall be those persons set out in the relevant entry in column (iii) of Appendix 3.

(2) In proceedings to which this Part applies a person may file a request in Form C2 that he or another person—

(*a*) be joined as a party, or

(*b*) cease to be a party.

(3) On considering a request under paragraph (2) the court shall, subject to paragraph (4)—

(*a*) grant it without a hearing or representations, save that this shall be done only in the case of a request under paragraph (2)(*a*), whereupon the proper officer or chief clerk shall inform the parties and the person making the request of that decision, or

(*b*) order that a date be fixed for the consideration of the request, whereupon the proper officer or chief clerk shall give notice of the date so fixed, together with a copy of the request—

   (i) in the case of a request under paragraph (2)(*a*), to the applicant, and

   (ii) in the case of a request under paragraph (2)(*b*), to the parties, or

(*c*) invite the parties or any of them to make written representations, within a specified period, as to whether the request should be granted; and upon the expiry of the period the court shall act in accordance with sub-paragraph (*a*) or (*b*).

(4) Where a person with parental responsibility requests that he be joined under paragraph (2)(*a*), the court shall grant his request.

(5) In proceedings to which this Part applies the court may direct—

(*a*) that a person who would not otherwise be a respondent under these rules be joined as a party to the proceedings, or

(*b*) that a party to the proceedings cease to be a party.

Service under this Part of the Rules

4.9.—(1) In proceedings to which this Part applies, the court may direct that a requirement of these rules to serve a document shall not apply or shall be effected in such manner as the court directs.

(2) Subject to the requirement in rule 4.7(1)(*b*) of personal service where service of a document is required under this Part it may be effected—

(*a*) if the person to be served is not known by the person serving to be acting by solicitor—

   (i) by delivering it to him personally, or

   (ii) by delivering it at, or by sending it by first class post to his residence or his last known residence, or

(*b*) if the person to be served is known by the person serving to be acting by solicitor—

   (i) by delivering the document at, or sending it by first class post to, the solicitor's address for service,

   (ii) where the solicitor's address for service includes a numbered box at a document exchange, by leaving the document at that document exchange or at a document exchange which transmits documents on every business day to that document exchange, or

   (iii) by sending a legible copy of the document by FAX (as defined by R.S.C. Order 1 rule 3(1)) in accordance with the provisions of R.S.C. Order 65 rule 5(2A) to the solicitor's office.

(3) Where a child who is a party to proceedings to which this Part applies is required by these rules to serve a document, service shall be effected by—

(a) the solicitor acting for the child, or

(b) where there is no such solicitor, the guardian ad litem, or

(c) where there is neither such a solicitor nor a guardian ad litem, the court.

(4) Service of any document on a child shall, subject to any direction of the court, be effected by service on—

(a) the solicitor acting for the child, or

(b) where there is no such solicitor, the guardian ad litem, or

(c) where there is neither such a solicitor nor a guardian ad litem, with leave of the court, the child.

(5) Where the court refuses leave under paragraph (3)(c) it shall give a direction under paragraph (1).

(6) A document shall, unless the contrary is proved, be deemed to have been served—

(a) in the case of service by first class post, on the second business day after posting, and

(b) in the case of service in accordance with paragraph (2)(b)(ii), on the second business day after the day on which it is left at the document exchange.

(7) At or before the first directions appointment in, or hearing of, proceedings to which this Part applies the applicant shall file a statement that service of—

(a) a copy of the application and other documents referred to in rule 4.5(1)(b) has been effected on each respondent, and

(b) notice of the proceedings has been given under rule 4.5(4);

and the statement shall indicate—

(i) the manner, date, time and place of service, or

(ii) where service was effected by post, the date, time and place of posting.

(8) In this rule "first class post" means first class post which has been pre-paid or in respect of which pre-payment is not required.

Answer to application

4.10.—(1) Within 14 days of service of an application for an Article 8 order or an application under Schedule 1, each respondent shall file and serve on the other parties an acknowledgement of the application in Form C4.

(2) Following service of an application to which this Part applies, other than an application under rule 4.4 or for an Article 8 order, a respondent may, subject to paragraph (3) file a written answer, which shall be served on the other parties.

(3) An answer under paragraph (2) shall, except in the case of an application under Articles 44, 50, 53, 57, 62, 63, 64, 67 and 69 be filed and served, not less than 2 days before the date fixed for the hearing of the application.

Appointment of guardian ad litem

4.11.—(1) As soon as practicable after the commencement of specified proceedings, or the transfer of such proceedings to the court, the court shall appoint a guardian ad litem, unless—

    (*a*) such an appointment has already been made by the court which made the transfer and is subsisting, or

    (*b*) the court considers that such an appointment is not necessary to safeguard the interests of the child.

(2) At any stage in specified proceedings a party may apply, without notice to the other parties unless the court directs otherwise, for the appointment of a guardian ad litem.

(3) The court shall grant an application under paragraph (2) unless it considers such an appointment not to be necessary to safeguard the interests of the child, in which case it shall give its reasons; and a note of such reasons shall be taken.

(4) At any stage in specified proceedings the court may, of its own motion, appoint a guardian ad litem.

(5) The proper officer or chief clerk shall, as soon as practicable, notify the parties and any welfare officer of an appointment under this rule or, as the case may be, of a decision not to make such an appointment.

(6) Upon the appointment of a guardian ad litem the proper officer or chief clerk shall, as soon as practicable, notify him of the appointment and serve on him copies of the application and of documents filed under rule 4.18(1).

(7) A guardian ad litem appointed from a panel established by regulations made under Article 60(7) shall not—

    (*a*) be a member, officer or servant of a Board or Trust which, or an authorised person (within the meaning of Article 49(2)) who, is a party to the proceedings;

    (*b*) be, or have been, a member, officer or servant of a Board or Trust or voluntary organisation (within the meaning of Article 74(1)) who has been directly concerned in that capacity in arrangements relating to the care, accommodation or welfare of the child during the 5 years prior to the commencement of the proceedings;

    (*c*) be a serving probation officer (except that a probation officer who has not in that capacity been previously concerned with the child or his family and who is employed part-time may, when not engaged in his duties as a probation officer, act as a guardian ad litem).

(8) When appointing a guardian ad litem the court may give consideration to appointing anyone who has previously acted as guardian ad litem of the same child.

(9) The appointment of a guardian ad litem under this rule shall continue for such time as is specified in the appointment or until terminated by the court.

(10) When terminating an appointment in accordance with paragraph (9), the court shall give its reasons in writing for doing so.

(11) Where the court appoints a guardian ad litem in accordance with this rule or refuses to make such an appointment or terminates an appointment the court shall record the appointment refusal or termination in Form C41.

Powers and duties of guardian ad litem

4.12.—(1) In carrying out his duty under Article 60(2), the guardian ad litem shall have regard to the principle set out in Article 3(2) and the matters set out in Article 3(3)(*a*) to (*f*) as if for the word "court" in that section there were substituted the words "guardian ad litem".

(2) The guardian ad litem shall—

(*a*) appoint a solicitor to represent the child unless such a solicitor has already been appointed, and

(*b*) give such advice to the child as is appropriate having regard to his understanding and, subject to rule 4.13(1)(*a*), instruct the solicitor representing the child on all matters relevant to the interests of the child, including possibilities for appeal, arising in the course of the proceedings.

(3) Where the guardian ad litem is the Official Solicitor, paragraph 2(*a*) shall not require him to appoint a solicitor for the child if he intends to act as the child's solicitor in the proceedings, unless—

(*a*) the child wishes to instruct a solicitor direct; and

(*b*) the Official Solicitor or the court considers that he is of sufficient understanding to do so.

(4) Where it appears to the guardian ad litem that the child—

(*a*) is instructing his solicitor direct, or

(*b*) intends to, and is capable of, conducting the proceedings on his own behalf,

he shall so inform the court and thereafter—

(i) shall perform all of his duties set out in this rule, other than duties under paragraph (2)(*a*) and such other duties as the court may direct,

(ii) shall take such part in the proceedings as the court may direct, and

(iii) may, with leave of the court, have legal representation in his conduct of those duties.

(5) The guardian ad litem shall, unless excused by the court, attend all directions appointments in and hearings of the proceedings and shall advise the court on the following matters—

(*a*) whether the child is of sufficient understanding for any purpose including the child's refusal to submit to a medical or psychiatric

56

examination or other assessment that the court has power to require, direct or order;

(b) the wishes of the child in respect of any matter relevant to the proceedings, including his attendance at court;

(c) the appropriate forum for the proceedings;

(d) the appropriate timing of the proceedings or any part of them;

(e) the options available to it in respect of the child and the suitability of each such option including what order should be made in determining the application;

(f) any other matter concerning which the court seeks his advice or concerning which he considers that the court should be informed.

(6) The advice given under paragraph (5) may, subject to any order of the court, be given orally or in writing; and if the advice be given orally, a note of it shall be taken.

(7) The guardian ad litem shall, where practicable, notify any person whose joinder as a party to those proceedings would be likely, in the guardian ad litem's opinion, to safeguard the interests of the child, of that person's right to apply to be joined under rule 4.8(2) and shall inform the court—

(a) of any such notification given,

(b) of anyone whom he attempted to notify under this paragraph but was unable to contact, and

(c) of anyone whom he believes may wish to be joined to the proceedings.

(8) The guardian ad litem shall, unless the court otherwise directs, not less than 7 days before the date fixed for the final hearing of the proceedings, file a written report advising on the interests of the child; and the proper officer or chief clerk shall, as soon as practicable, serve a copy of the report on the parties.

(9) The guardian ad litem shall serve and accept service of documents on behalf of the child in accordance with rule 4.9(2)(b) and (3)(b) and, where the child has not himself been served, and has sufficient understanding, advise the child of the contents of any document so served.

(10) The guardian ad litem shall make such investigations as may be necessary for him to carry out his duties and shall, in particular—

(a) contact or seek to interview such persons as he thinks appropriate or as the court directs,

(b) if he inspects records of the kinds referred to in Article 61, bring to the attention of the court and such other persons as the court may direct all such records and documents which may, in his opinion, assist in the proper determination of the proceedings, and

(c) obtain such professional assistance as is available to him which he thinks appropriate or which the court directs him to obtain.

(11) In addition to his duties under other paragraphs of this rule, the guardian ad litem shall provide to the court such other assistance as it may require.

(12) A party may question the guardian ad litem about oral or written advice tendered by him to the court under this rule.

Solicitor for child

4.13.—(1) A solicitor appointed under Article 60(3) or in accordance with rule 4.12(2)(*a*) shall represent the child—

(*a*) in accordance with instructions received from the guardian ad litem (unless the solicitor considers, having taken into account the views of the guardian ad litem and any direction of the court under rule 4.12(4), that the child wishes to give instructions which conflict with those of the guardian ad litem and that he is able, having regard to his understanding, to give such instructions on his own behalf in which case he shall conduct the proceedings in accordance with instructions received from the child) or

(*b*) where no guardian ad litem has been appointed for the child and the condition in Article 60(4)(*b*) is satisfied, in accordance with instructions received from the child, or

(*c*) in default of instructions under (*a*) or (*b*), in furtherance of the best interests of the child.

(2) A solicitor appointed under Article 60(3) or in accordance with rule 4.12(2)(*a*) shall serve and accept service of documents on behalf of the child in accordance with rule 4.9(2)(*a*) and (3)(*a*), and, where the child has not himself been served and has sufficient understanding, advise the child of the contents of any document so served.

(3) Where the child wishes an appointment of a solicitor under Article 60(3) or in accordance with rule 4.12(2)(*a*) to be terminated, he may apply to the court for an order terminating the appointment; and the solicitor and the guardian ad litem shall be given an opportunity to make representations.

(4) Where the guardian ad litem wishes an appointment of a solicitor under Article 60(3) to be terminated, he may apply to the court for an order terminating the appointment; and the solicitor and, if he is of sufficient understanding, the child, shall be given an opportunity to make representations.

(5) When terminating an appointment in accordance with paragraph (3) or (4), the court shall give its reasons for so doing, a note of which shall be taken.

(6) Where the court appoints a solicitor under Article 60(3) or refuses to make such an appointment or terminates an appointment, the court or the proper officer or chief clerk shall record the appointment refusal or termination in Form C42.

Welfare officer

4.14.—(1) Where the court has directed that a written report be made by a welfare officer, the report shall be filed at or by such time as the court directs or, in the absence of such a direction, at least 14 days before a relevant hearing; and the proper officer or chief clerk shall, as soon as practicable, serve a copy of the report on the parties and any guardian ad litem.

(2) In paragraph (1), a hearing is relevant if the proper officer or chief clerk has given the welfare officer notice that his report is to be considered at it.

(3) After the filing of a report by a welfare officer, the court may direct that the welfare officer attend any hearing at which the report is to be considered; and

(a) except where such a direction is given at a hearing attended by the welfare officer, the proper officer or chief clerk shall inform the welfare officer of the direction; and

(b) at the hearing at which the report is considered any party may question the welfare officer about his report.

(4) This rule is without prejudice to any power to give directions under rule 4.15.

Directions

4.15.—(1) In this rule, "party" includes the guardian ad litem and, where a request or a direction concerns a report under Article 4, the welfare officer.

(2) In proceedings to which this Part applies the court may, subject to paragraph (3), give, vary or revoke directions for the conduct of the proceedings, including—

(a) the timetable for the proceedings;

(b) varying the time within which or by which an act is required, by these rules or by other rules of court, to be done;

(c) the attendance of the child;

(d) the appointment of a guardian ad litem, whether under Article 60 or otherwise, or of a solicitor under Article 60(3);

(e) the service of documents;

(f) the submission of evidence including experts' reports;

(g) the preparation of welfare reports under Article 4;

(h) the transfer of the proceedings to another court;

(i) consolidation with other proceedings.

(3) Directions under paragraph (2) may be given, varied or revoked either—

(a) of the court's own motion having given the parties notice of its intention to do so and an opportunity to attend and be heard or to make written representations,

(b) on the written request in Form C2 of a party specifying the direction which is sought, filed and served on the other parties, or

(c) on the written request in Form C2 of a party specifying the direction which is sought, to which the other parties consent and which they or their representatives have signed.

(4) In an urgent case the request under paragraph (3)(b) may, with the leave of the court, be made—

(*a*) orally, or

(*b*) without notice to the parties, or

(*c*) both as in sub-paragraph (*a*) and as in sub-paragraph (*b*).

(5) On receipt of a written request under paragraph (3)(*b*) the proper officer or chief clerk shall fix a date for the hearing of the request and give not less than 2 days' notice in Form C3 to the parties of the date so fixed.

(6) On considering a request under paragraph (3)(*c*) the court shall either—

(*a*) grant the request, whereupon the proper officer or chief clerk shall inform the parties of the decision, or

(*b*) direct that a date be fixed for the hearing of the request, whereupon the proper officer or chief clerk shall fix such a date and give not less than 2 days' notice in Form C3 to the parties of the date so fixed.

(7) A party may apply in accordance with paragraph 3(*b*) or (*c*) for an order to be made under Article 11(3) or, if he is entitled to apply for such an order, under Article 57(1) and paragraphs (4), (5) and (6) shall apply accordingly.

(8) Where a court is considering making, of its own motion, an Article 8 order, or an order under Article 50, 53 or 57, the power to give directions under paragraph (2) shall apply.

(9) Directions of a court which are still in force immediately prior to the transfer of proceedings to which this Part applies to another court shall continue to apply following the transfer, subject to any changes of terminology which are required to apply those directions to the court to which the proceedings are transferred, unless varied or discharged by directions under paragraph (2).

(10) The court shall take a note of the giving, variation or revocation of a direction under this rule and serve, as soon as practicable, a copy of the note on any party who was not present at the giving, variation or revocation.

Timing of proceedings

4.16.—(1) Where these rules or other rules of court provide a time period within which or by which a certain act is to be performed in the course of proceedings to which this Part applies, that period may not be extended otherwise than by direction of the court under rule 4.15.

(2) At the—

(*a*) postponement or adjournment of any hearing or directions appointment in the course of proceedings to which this Part applies, or

(*b*) conclusion of any such hearing or directions appointment other than one at which the proceedings are determined, or so soon thereafter as is practicable, the court shall fix a date upon which the proceedings shall come before the court again for such purposes as the court directs; and the proper officer or chief clerk shall give notice to the parties, and to any guardian ad litem or welfare officer of the date fixed.

(3) At the transfer to a court of proceedings to which this Part applies the court to which the proceedings are transferred shall as soon as possible fix a date upon which the proceedings shall come before the court for such purposes as the court directs; and the proper officer or chief clerk shall give notice to the parties and to any guardian ad litem or welfare officer of the date so fixed.

Attendance at a directions appointment and hearing

4.17.—(1) Subject to paragraph (2), a party shall attend a directions appointment of which he has been given notice in accordance with rule 4.15(5) unless the court otherwise directs.

(2) Proceedings or any part of them shall take place in the absence of any party, including the child, if—

    (*a*) the court considers it in the interests of the child, having regard to the matters to be discussed or the evidence likely to be given, and

    (*b*) the party is represented by a guardian ad litem or solicitor;

and when considering the interests of the child under sub-paragraph (*a*) the court shall give the guardian ad litem, the solicitor for the child and, if he is of sufficient understanding, the child an opportunity to make representations.

(3) Subject to paragraph (4), where at the time and place appointed for a hearing or directions appointment the applicant appears but one or more of the respondents do not, the court may proceed with the hearing or appointment.

(4) The court shall not begin to hear an application in the absence of a respondent unless—

    (*a*) it is proved to the satisfaction of the court that he received reasonable notice of the date of the hearing; or

    (*b*) the court is satisfied that the circumstances of the case justify proceeding with the hearing.

(5) Where, at the time and place appointed for a hearing or directions appointment one or more of the respondents appear but the applicant does not, the court may refuse the application or, if sufficient evidence has previously been received, proceed in the absence of the applicant.

(6) Where at the time and place appointed for a hearing or directions appointment neither the applicant nor any respondent appears, the court may refuse the application.

Documentary evidence

4.18.—(1) Subject to paragraphs (4) and (5), in proceedings to which this Part applies a party shall file and serve on the parties, any welfare officer and any guardian ad litem of whose appointment he has been given notice under rule 4.11(5)—

(*a*) written statements of the substance of the oral evidence which the party intends to adduce at a hearing of, or a directions appointment in, those proceedings, which shall—

    (i) be dated,

    (ii) be signed by the person making the statement,

    (iii) contain a declaration that the maker of the statement believes it to be true and understands that it may be placed before the court; and

    (iv) show in the top right-hand corner of the first page—

        (*a*) the initials and surname of the person making the statement,

        (*b*) the number of the statement in relation to the maker,

        (*c*) the date on which the statement was made, and

        (*d*) the party on whose behalf it is filed; and

(*b*) copies of any documents, including experts' reports, upon which the party intends to rely at a hearing of, or a directions appointment in, those proceedings,

at or by such time as the court directs or, in the absence of a direction, before the hearing or appointment.

(2) A party may, subject to any direction of the court about the timing of statements under this rule, file and serve on the parties a statement which is supplementary to a statement served under paragraph (1).

(3) At a hearing or a directions appointment a party may not, without the leave of the court—

(*a*) adduce evidence, or

(*b*) seek to rely on a document,

in respect of which he has failed to comply with the requirements of paragraph (1).

(4) In proceedings for an Article 8 order a party shall—

(*a*) neither file nor serve any document other than as required or authorised by these rules, and

(*b*) in completing a form prescribed by these rules, neither give information, nor make a statement, which is not required or authorised by that form,

without the leave of the court.

(5) In proceedings for an Article 8 order no statement or copy may be filed under paragraph (1) until such time as the court directs.

Expert evidence — examination of child

4.19.—(1) No person may, without the leave of the court, cause the child to be medically or psychiatrically examined, or otherwise assessed, for the purpose of the preparation of expert evidence for use in the proceedings.

(2) An application for leave under paragraph (1) shall be made in Form C2 and shall, unless the court otherwise directs be served on all parties to the proceedings and on the guardian ad litem.

(3) Where the leave of the court has not been given under paragraph (1), no evidence arising out of an examination or assessment to which that paragraph applies may be adduced without the leave of the court.

Amendment

4.20.—(1) Subject to rule 4.18(2) a document which has been filed or served in proceedings to which this Part applies, may not be amended without the leave of the court which shall, unless the court otherwise directs, be requested in writing.

(2) On considering a request for leave to amend a document the court shall either—

(*a*) grant the request, whereupon the proper officer or chief clerk shall inform the person making the request of that decision, or

(*b*) invite the parties or any of them to make representations, within a specified period, as to whether such an order should be made.

(3) A person amending a document shall file it and serve it on those persons on whom it was served prior to amendment and the amendments shall be identified.

Hearing

4.21.—(1) The court may give directions as to the order of speeches and evidence at a hearing or directions appointment, in the course of proceedings to which this Part applies.

(2) Subject to directions under paragraph (1), at a hearing of, or directions appointment in, proceedings to which this Part applies, the parties and the guardian ad litem shall adduce their evidence in the following order—

(*a*) the applicant,

(*b*) any party with parental responsibility for the child,

(*c*) other respondents,

(*d*) the guardian ad litem,

(*e*) the child, if he is a party to the proceedings and there is no guardian ad litem.

(3) After the final hearing of proceedings to which this Part applies, the court shall deliver its judgment as soon as is practicable.

(4) When making an order or when refusing an application, the court shall either—

(*a*) issue a written judgment;

(*b*) cause the judgment to be recorded by mechanical or electronic means; or

(*c*) record in Form C19 any finding of fact which it made and the reasons for its decision.

(5) An order made in proceedings to which this Part applies shall be recorded either in the appropriate form in Appendix 1 to these rules or, where there is no such form, in writing.

(6) A copy of an order made in accordance with paragraph (5) shall, as soon as practicable after it has been made, be served by the proper officer or chief clerk on the parties to the proceedings in which it was made and on any person with whom the child is living.

Attachment of penal notice to Article 8 order

4.22. C.C.R. Order 57 rule 7 shall apply to Article 8 orders as if for paragraph (1) of that rule there were substituted the following—

"(1) In the case of an Article 8 order (within the meaning of Article 8(2) of the Children (Northern Ireland) Order 1995) enforceable by committal order under rule 5 the judge or the district judge may, on the application of the person entitled to enforce the order, direct the chief clerk to issue a copy of the order endorsed with a notice in Form 270 and the copy so endorsed shall be served on the respondent personally and no copy of the order shall be issued with any such notice endorsed save in accordance with such direction.".

Appeals

4.23.—(1) Where an appeal lies—

(*a*) to the High Court; or

(*b*) to a county court specified in the Allocation Order for the purposes of Article 166(4)(*a*) of the Order of 1995 against the making or refusal to make an order under the Order of 1995—

it shall be made in accordance with the following provisions and references to "the court below" are references to the court from which the appeal lies.

(2) The appellant shall file and serve on the parties to the proceedings in the court below, and on any guardian ad litem—

(*a*) notice of the appeal in writing, setting out the grounds upon which he relies;

(*b*) a certified copy of the summons or application and of the order appealed against, and of any order staying its execution;

(*c*) a copy of any reasons given for the decision.

(3) The notice of appeal shall be filed and served in accordance with paragraph (2)(*a*)—

(*a*) within 14 days after the determination against which the appeal is brought, or

(*b*) in the case of an appeal against an order under Article 57(1), within 7 days after the making of the order, or

(*c*) with the leave of the court to which the appeal is to be brought, within such other time as that court may direct.

(4) The documents mentioned in paragraph (2)(*b*) to (*c*) shall, subject to any direction of the court to which the appeal is to be brought, be filed and served as soon as practicable after the filing and service of the notice of appeal under paragraph (2)(*a*).

(5) The applicant shall also send a copy of the notice of appeal to the chief clerk or, as the case may be, to the clerk of petty sessions of the court below.

(6) Subject to paragraph (7), a respondent who wishes—

(*a*) to contend on the appeal that the decision of the court below should be varied, either in any event or in the event of the appeal being allowed in whole or in part, or

(*b*) to contend that the decision of the court below should be affirmed on grounds other than those relied upon by that court, or

(*c*) to contend by way of cross-appeal that the decision of the court below was wrong in whole or in part,

shall, within 14 days of receipt of notice of the appeal, file and serve on all other parties to the appeal a notice in writing, setting out the grounds upon which he relies.

(7) No notice under paragraph (5) may be filed or served in an appeal against an order under Article 57.

Confidentiality of documents

4.24.—(1) Notwithstanding any rule of court to the contrary, no document, other than a record of an order, held by the court and relating to proceedings to which this Part applies shall be disclosed, other than to—

(*a*) a party,

(*b*) the legal representative of a party,

(*c*) the guardian ad litem,

(*d*) the Legal Aid Department, or

(*e*) a welfare officer

without leave of the judge.

(2) An application for leave shall be made in Form C2 setting out the reasons for the request.

(3) Nothing in this rule shall prevent the notification by the court or the proper officer or chief clerk of a direction under Article 56(1) to the authority concerned.

Notification of consent

4.25. Consent for the purposes of Article 16(3) or 33(3)(*c*) or (*d*) shall be given either—

(*a*) orally in court, or

(*b*) in writing to the court signed by the person giving his consent.

Secure accommodation

4.26. In proceedings under Article 44, the court shall, if practicable, arrange for copies of all written reports before it to be made available before the hearing to—

(*a*) the applicant,

(*b*) the parent or guardian of the child,

(*c*) any legal representative of the child,

(*d*) the guardian ad litem; and

(*e*) the child, unless the court otherwise directs

and copies of such reports may, if the court considers it desirable, be shown to any person who is entitled to notice of the proceedings in accordance with these rules.

Investigation under Article 56

4.27.—(1) This rule applies where a direction is given to an appropriate authority by the High Court or a county court under Article 56(1).

(2) On giving a direction the court shall adjourn the proceedings and shall record the direction in Form C35.

(3) A copy of the direction recorded under paragraph (2) shall, as soon as practicable after the direction is given, be served by the proper officer or chief clerk on the parties to the proceedings in which the direction is given and, where the appropriate authority is not a party, on that authority.

(4) When serving the copy of the direction on the appropriate authority the proper officer or chief clerk shall also serve copies of such of the documentary evidence which has been, or is to be, adduced in the proceedings as the court may direct.

(5) Where an authority informs the court of any of the matters set out in Article 56(3)(*a*) to (*c*) it shall do so in writing.

PART V

APPEALS

Appeal from a divorce county court to the Court of Appeal

5.1. R.S.C. Order 58 rule 4 and Order 59 shall apply with the necessary modifications to an appeal to the Court of Appeal under Article 48(9) of the Order of 1978(**a**) or Article 40(2) of or paragraph 10 of Schedule 1 to the Order of 1989 from a decree or order of a judge in divorce county court proceedings as if the reference to the High Court in Order 59 rule 10(1) were a reference to a divorce county court.

Appeal from the district judge

5.2.—(1) C.C.R. Order 14 rule 1(1)(*f*) (which enables the judge to vary or rescind an order by the district judge in the course of proceedings) shall not apply to an order or decision made or given by the district judge in family proceedings in a county court but any party may appeal from such an order or decision to a judge on notice filed within 5 days after the order or decision was made or given and served not later than 2 clear days before the day fixed for hearing of the appeal, which shall be heard in chambers unless the judge otherwise orders.

(**a**) S.I. 1978/1045 (N.I. 15) as amended by Article 185(1) and paragraph 96 of Schedule 9 to the Children (Northern Ireland) Order 1995 (S.I. 1995/755 (N.I. 2))

(2) Except so far as the court may otherwise order, an appeal under paragraph (1) shall not operate as a stay of proceedings on the order or decision appealed from.

PART VI

DISABILITY

Interpretation

6.1.—(1) In this Part—

"person under disability" means a person who is a minor or a person who by reason of mental disorder within the meaning of the Mental Health (Northern Ireland) Order 1986**(a)** is incapable of managing and administering his property and affairs.

(2) So far as they relate to minors who are the subject of applications the provisions of this Part shall not apply to proceedings which are specified proceedings within the meaning of Article 60(6) of the Order of 1995 and this Part shall have effect subject to the said Article 60(6) and Part IV.

(3) Rule 6.3 shall apply only to proceedings under the Order of 1995.

Person under disability must sue by next friend etc

6.2.—(1) A person under disability may begin and prosecute any family proceedings by his next friend and may defend any such proceedings by his guardian ad litem and, except as otherwise provided by this rule, it shall not be necessary for a guardian ad litem to be appointed by the court.

(2) No person's name shall be used in any proceedings as next friend of a person under disability unless he is the Official Solicitor or the documents mentioned in paragraph (6) have been filed.

(3) Where the disability of a person who is entitled to defend any family proceedings is not solely due to minority, the Official Solicitor shall, if he consents, be guardian ad litem; but at any stage of the proceedings an application may be made (on not less than 4 days' notice to the Official Solicitor, if he has consented to act) for the appointment of some other person as guardian; and there shall be filed in support of any application under this paragraph the documents mentioned in paragraph (6).

(4) Where a petition, answer, application or originating summons has been served on a person whom there is reasonable ground for believing to be a person under disability and no notice of intention to defend has been given or answer or affidavit in answer filed on his behalf, the party at whose instance the document was served shall, before taking any further step in the proceedings, apply to the Master for directions as to whether a guardian ad litem should be appointed to act for that person in the cause, and on any such application the Master may, if he considers it necessary in order to protect the interest of the person served, order that some proper person be appointed his guardian ad litem.

(a) S.I. 1986/595 (N.I. 4)

(5) No notice of intention to defend shall be given, or answer or affidavit in answer filed (by or on behalf of a person under disability) unless the person giving the notice or filing the answer or affidavit—

(a) is the Official Solicitor or, in a case in which paragraph (3) applies, is the Official Solicitor or has been appointed by the court to be guardian ad litem; or

(b) in any other case, has filed the documents mentioned in paragraph (6).

(6) The documents referred to in paragraphs (2), (3) and (5) are—

(a) a written consent to act by the proposed next friend or guardian ad litem;

(b) a certificate by the solicitor acting for the person under disability—

(i) that he knows or believes that the person to whom the certificate relates is a person under disability stating the grounds of his knowledge or belief, and

(ii) that the person named in the certificate as next friend or guardian ad litem has no interest in the cause or matter in question adverse to that of the person under disability and is a proper person to be next friend or guardian.

Certain minors may sue without next friend etc

6.3.—(1) Where a person entitled to begin, prosecute or defend any proceedings to which this rule applies, is a minor to whom this Part applies, he may subject to paragraph (3), begin, prosecute or defend, as the case may be, such proceedings without a next friend or guardian ad litem—

(a) where he has obtained the leave of the court for that purpose; or

(b) where a solicitor—

(i) considers that the minor is able, having regard to his understanding, to give instructions in relation to the proceedings; and

(ii) has accepted instructions from the minor to act for him in the proceedings and, where the proceedings have begun, is so acting.

(2) A minor shall be entitled to apply for the leave of the court under paragraph (1)(a) without a next friend or guardian ad litem either—

(a) by filing a written request for leave setting out the reasons for the application, or

(b) by making an oral request for leave at any hearing in the proceedings.

(3) On considering a request for leave filed under paragraph (2)(a), the court shall either—

(a) grant the request, whereupon the proper officer or chief clerk shall communicate the decision to the minor and, where the leave relates to the prosecution or defence of existing proceedings, to the other parties to those proceedings, or

(b) direct that the request be heard ex parte, whereupon the proper officer or chief clerk shall fix a date for such a hearing and give to the minor making the request such notice of the date so fixed as the court may direct.

(4) Where a minor has a next friend or guardian ad litem in proceedings and the minor wishes to prosecute or defend the remaining stages of the proceedings without a next friend or guardian ad litem, the minor may apply to the court for leave for that purpose and for the removal of the next friend or guardian ad litem; and paragraph (2) shall apply to the application as if it were an application under paragraph (1)(*a*).

(5) On considering a request filed under paragraph (2) by virtue of paragraph (4), the court shall either—

(*a*) grant the request, whereupon the proper officer or chief clerk shall communicate the decision to the minor and next friend or guardian ad litem concerned and to all other parties to the proceedings, or

(*b*) direct that the request be heard, whereupon the proper officer or chief clerk shall fix a date for such a hearing and give to the minor and next friend or guardian ad litem concerned such notice of the date so fixed as the court may direct;

provided that the court may act under sub-paragraph (*a*) only if it is satisfied that the next friend or guardian ad litem does not oppose the request.

(6) Where the court is considering whether to—

(*a*) grant leave under paragraph (1)(*a*), or

(*b*) grant leave under paragraph (4) and remove a next friend or guardian ad litem,

it shall grant the leave sought and, as the case may be, remove the next friend or guardian ad litem if it considers that the minor concerned has sufficient understanding to participate as a party in the proceedings concerned or proposed without a next friend or guardian ad litem.

(7) Where a request for leave is granted at a hearing fixed under paragraph (3)(*b*) (in relation to the prosecution or defence of proceedings already begun) or (5)(*b*), the proper officer or chief clerk shall forthwith communicate the decision to the other parties to the proceedings.

(8) The court may revoke any leave granted under paragraph (1)(*a*) where it considers that the child does not have sufficient understanding to participate as a party in the proceedings concerned without a next friend or guardian ad litem.

(9) Without prejudice to any requirement of C.C.R. Order 43, rule 2 or R.S.C. Order 67, where a solicitor is acting for a minor in proceedings which the minor is prosecuting or defending without a next friend or guardian ad litem by virtue of paragraph (1)(*b*) and either of the conditions specified in the paragraph (1)(*b*)(i) and (ii) cease to be fulfilled, he shall forthwith so inform the court.

(10) Where—

(*a*) the court revokes any leave under paragraph (8), or

(*b*) either of the conditions specified in paragraph (1)(*b*)(i) and (ii) is no longer fulfilled, the court may, if it considers it necessary in order to protect the interests of the minor concerned, order that some proper person be appointed his next friend or guardian ad litem.

(11) Where a minor is of sufficient understanding to begin, prosecute or defend proceedings without a next friend or guardian ad litem—

(a) he may nevertheless begin, prosecute or defend them by his next friend or guardian ad litem; and

(b) where he is prosecuting or defending proceedings by his next friend or guardian ad litem, the respective powers and duties of the minor and next friend or guardian ad litem, except those conferred or imposed by this rule shall not be affected by the minor's ability to dispense with a next friend or guardian ad litem under the provisions of this rule.

Service on person under disability

6.4.—(1) Where a document to which rule 2.9 applies is required to be served on a person under disability it shall be served—

(a) in the case of a minor who is not otherwise a person under disability, on his father or guardian or, if he has no father or guardian, on the person with whom he resides or in whose care he is;

(b) in the case of any other person under disability—

(i) on the Official Solicitor if he has consented under rule 6.2(3) to be the guardian ad litem, or

(ii) if the Official Solicitor has not so consented, on the person with whom he resides or in whose care he is:

Provided that the court may order that a document which has been, or is to be, served on the person under disability or on a person other than one mentioned in sub-paragraph (a) or (b) shall be deemed to be duly served on the person under disability.

(2) Where a document is served in accordance with paragraph (1), it shall be indorsed with a notice in Form M22; and after service has been effected the person at whose instance the document was served shall, unless the Official Solicitor is the guardian ad litem of the person under disability or the court otherwise directs, file an affidavit by the person on whom the document was served stating whether the contents of the document were, or its purport was, communicated to the person under disability and, if not, the reasons for not doing so.

Petition for nullity on ground of insanity, etc

6.5.—(1) Where a petition for nullity has been presented on the ground that at the time of the marriage the respondent was suffering from mental disorder within the meaning of the Mental Health (Northern Ireland) Order 1986 of such a kind or to such an extent as to be unfitted for marriage, then, whether or not the respondent gives notice of intention to defend, the petitioner shall not proceed with the cause without the leave of the Master.

(2) The Master may make it a condition of granting leave that some proper person be appointed to act as guardian ad litem of the respondent.

Separate representation of children

6.6.—(1) Without prejudice to rule 2.59, if in any family proceedings it appears to the court that any child ought to be separately represented, the court may appoint—

(*a*) the Official Solicitor, or

(*b*) some other proper person

(provided, in either case, that he consents) to be the guardian ad litem of the child, with authority to take part in the proceedings on the child's behalf.

(2) An order under paragraph (1) may be made by the court of its own motion or on the application of a party to the proceedings or of the proposed guardian ad litem.

(3) The court may at any time direct that an application be made by a party for an order under paragraph (1) and may stay the proceedings until the application has been made.

(4) Unless the court otherwise directs, on making an application for an order under paragraph (1) the applicant shall—

(*a*) unless he is the proposed guardian ad litem, file a written consent by the proposed guardian to act as such;

(*b*) unless the proposed guardian ad litem is the Official Solicitor, file a certificate that the proposed guardian has no interest in the proceedings adverse to that of the child and is a proper person to be guardian.

(5) Unless the court otherwise directs, a person appointed under this rule or rule 2.59 to be the guardian ad litem of a child in any family proceedings shall be treated as a party for the purpose of any provision of these Rules requiring a document to be served on or notice to be given to a party to the proceedings.

PART VII

PROCEDURE

Application

7.1. Except for rule 7.2, the provisions of this Part apply to all family proceedings, but have effect subject to the provisions of any other Part of these Rules.

Security for costs in a matrimonial cause

7.2.—(1) A wife who is petitioner in a cause or who has given notice of intention to defend may, after the certificate of readiness has been lodged or at an earlier stage of a cause with leave, lodge her bill of costs incurred to the date of such certificate for taxation against her husband. The taxing master on the taxation of such bill of costs shall if requested by the wife so to do ascertain what is a sufficient sum of money to cover the costs of the wife of and incidental to the trial or hearing of the cause, and the Master may, unless the husband shall prove that the wife has sufficient separate estate or show other good cause, order the husband within such time as the Master may fix to pay to the wife or into court the amount of such taxed costs and to pay into court or secure the sum ascertained as sufficient to cover the costs of and incidental to the trial or hearing and may direct a stay of the proceedings until the order is complied with.

(2) C.C.R. Order 4, rule 1 (which provides that a plaintiff may be required to give security for costs if he is not resident in Northern Ireland), shall not apply to matrimonial proceedings in a county court.

Service out of Northern Ireland

7.3.—(1) Any document in family proceedings may be served out of the jurisdiction without leave either in the manner prescribed by these Rules for service within the jurisdiction or in accordance with R.S.C. Order 11.

(2) Where a petition or notice of an application for ancillary relief is to be served out of the jurisdiction, the time limited for giving notice of intention to defend which is to be endorsed on the petition or contained in the notice shall be fixed having regard to the place where or country within which the petition or notice is to be served in accordance with the practice adopted under the said Order.

Service of documents

7.4.—(1) Where a document is required by these Rules to be sent to any person, it shall, unless otherwise directed, be sent by post—

(*a*) if a solicitor is acting for him,

   (i) to the solicitor's address; or

  (ii) where that address includes a numbered box at a document exchange, at that document exchange or at a document exchange which transmits documents every business day to that document exchange; and any document which is left at a document exchange in accordance with this paragraph, shall unless the contrary is proved, be deemed to have been served on the second business day following the day on which it is left;

 (iii) by sending a legible copy of the document by FAX (as defined by R.S.C. Order 1 rule 3(1)) in accordance with the provisions of R.S.C. Order 65 rule 5(2A) to the solicitor's office;

(*b*) if he is acting in person, to the address for service given by him or, if he has not given an address for service his last known address, but if in the opinion of the Master the document would be unlikely to reach him if sent to that address, the Master may dispense with sending the document to him.

(2) Unless the court otherwise directs, service of any document in family proceedings shall, if no other mode of service is prescribed or ordered, be effected—

(*a*) if a solicitor is acting for the person to be served by leaving the document at, or sending it by first class pre-paid post to, the solicitor's address;

(*b*) if the person to be served is acting in person, by delivering the document to him or by leaving it at, or sending it by first class pre-paid post to, the address for service given by him or, if he has not given an address for service, his last known address;

Provided that where, in a case to which sub-paragraph (*b*) applies, it appears to the Master that it is impracticable to deliver the documents to the person to be served and that, if the document were left at, or sent by post to, the address specified in that sub-paragraph, it would be unlikely to reach him, the Master may dispense with service of the document.

Mode of making applications

7.5. Except where these Rules, or any rules applied by these Rules, otherwise provide, every application in family proceedings shall be made to a Master by summons.

No notice of intention to proceed after year's delay

7.6. No provision in the Rules of the Supreme Court (Northern Ireland) 1980, which requires a party to give notice of intention to proceed after a year's delay, shall apply to any family proceedings.

Filing of documents at place of hearing, etc

7.7. Where the file of any matrimonial proceedings has been sent from the Matrimonial Office to a county court for the purpose of a hearing or for some other purpose, any document required to be filed shall be filed in that court.

Mode of giving notice

7.8. Unless the court otherwise directs, any notice which is required by these Rules to be given to any person shall be in writing and, if it is to be given by the proper officer or chief clerk, shall be given by post.

Copies of Decrees and Order

7.9.—(1) A copy of every decree or order shall be sent by the proper officer or chief clerk to every party to the cause.

(2) A sealed or other copy of a decree or order pronounced or made in open court shall be issued to any person requiring it on payment of the prescribed fee.

Service of order

7.10.—(1) Where an order made in family proceedings has been drawn up, the proper officer or chief clerk, as the case may be, shall, unless the court otherwise directs, send a copy of the order to every party affected by it.

(2) Where a party against whom the order is made is acting by a solicitor, a copy may, if the Master thinks fit, be sent to that party as well as to his solicitor.

(3) It shall not be necessary for the person in whose favour the order was made to prove that a copy of the order has reached any other party to whom it is required to be sent.

(4) This rule is without prejudice to R.S.C. Order 45, rule 5 (which deals with the service of an order to do or abstain from doing an act), C.C.R. Order 57, rule 7 (which deals with orders enforceable by attachment), and any other rule or enactment for the purposes of which an order is required to be served in a particular way.

Record of proceedings at trial

7.11.—(1) A record of the proceedings at the trial of every cause shall where practicable be made by mechanical or electronic means.

(2) A record may be made by mechanical or electronic means of any other proceedings before the judge if directions for making such a record are given by him.

(3) The person who operated the recording machine shall, if it be the case, certify that the recording is a complete recording or a continuous part of a complete recording taken at the proceedings to which it relates.

(4) On being so directed a shorthand writer or other competent person shall furnish the Master with a transcript of the whole or such part as may be directed of the record.

(5) The shorthand writer or other competent person shall, if it be the case, certify the transcript to be a correct transcript of the record or such part of the record as may be requested.

(6) Any party, any person who has intervened in a cause or the Crown Solicitor shall be entitled to bespeak a copy of the transcript on payment of the appropriate fee.

Inspection of documents retained in court

7.12.—(1) A party to any family proceedings or his solicitor or the Crown Solicitor or a person appointed under rule 2.59 or 6.6 to be the guardian ad litem of a child in any family proceedings may have a search made for, and may inspect and bespeak a copy of, any document filed or lodged in the court office in those proceedings.

(2) Except as provided by paragraph (1) of this rule no document filed or lodged in the court office other than a decree or order made in open court, shall be open to inspection by any person without the leave of the Master, and no copy of any such document, or of an extract from any such document, shall be taken by, or issued to, any person without such leave.

Disclosure of information under the Order of 1991

7.13. Where the Department requires a person mentioned in regulation 2(2) or (3) of the Child Support (Information, Evidence and Disclosure)

Regulations (Northern Ireland) 1992(a) to furnish information or evidence for a purpose mentioned in regulation 3 of those Regulations nothing in rule 7.12 shall prevent that person from furnishing the information or evidence sought or require him to seek the leave of the court before doing so.

Applications for relief which are precluded by the Order of 1991

7.14.—(1) Where an application is made for an order which in the opinion of the Master, the court would be prevented from making by Article 10 or 11 of the Order of 1991 the proper officer or chief clerk as the case may be, shall send a notice in Form M31 to the applicant and to the other parties.

(2) In the first instance, the Master shall consider the matter under paragraph (1), without holding a hearing.

(3) An applicant who has been sent a notice under paragraph (1) may within 14 days of receipt of the notice inform the proper officer or chief clerk, as the case may be, in writing, that he wishes to pursue his application and upon being so informed the proper officer shall act in accordance with paragraph (4) and the chief clerk shall refer the matter to the district judge who shall act in accordance with paragraph (4).

(4) Where the Master acts in accordance with this paragraph he shall fix an appointment for the matter to be heard and determined by the court and may direct that the hearing shall be ex parte.

(5) Where an appointment has been fixed in accordance with paragraph (4) the proper officer or chief clerk, as the case may be, shall give the applicant notice of the date and time of the appointment and in relation to the other parties—

(a) where the hearing is to be ex parte, inform them that the matter is being resolved ex parte and that they will be informed of the result in due course;

(b) where the hearing is to be inter partes, inform them of the date and time of the appointment.

(6) Where a notice is sent under paragraph (1) and the proper officer or chief clerk, as the case may be, is not informed under paragraph (3) the application shall be treated as having been withdrawn.

(7) Where the matter is heard in accordance with paragraph (4) and the court determines that it would be prevented by Article 10 or 11 of the Order of 1991 from making the order sought it shall dismiss the application.

(8) Where the court dismisses an application under this rule it shall give its reasons in writing, copies of which shall be sent to the parties by the proper officer or chief clerk, as the case may be.

(9) In this rule "the matter" means the question whether the making of an order in the terms sought by the application would be prevented by Article 10 or 11 of the Order of 1991.

(a) S.R. 1992 No. 339

Additional requirement where application for child maintenance is combined with application for other relief

7.15. Where a notice is sent under rule 7.14(1) in respect of an application which is contained in a petition or other document ("the document") which contains material intrinsic to the application—

(a) the document shall, until the contrary is directed under sub-paragraph (c), be treated as if it did not contain the application in respect of which the notice was sent;

(b) the proper officer or chief clerk shall, when he sends a copy of the notice under rule 7.14(1) to the parties, also send a notice informing them of the effect of sub-paragraph (a); and

(c) where it is determined under rule 7.14 that the court would not be prevented by Article 10 or 11 of the Order of 1991 from making the order sought by the application, the court shall direct that the document shall be treated as if it contained the application, and it may give such directions as it considers appropriate for the conduct of the proceedings in consequence of that direction.

Disclosure of address

7.16.—(1) Subject to rule 2.4 nothing in these Rules shall be construed as requiring any party to reveal the address of their private residence (or that of any child) except by order of the court.

(2) Where a party declines to reveal an address in reliance upon paragraph (1) he shall give notice to the court in Form C5 and that address shall not be revealed to any person except by order of the court.

Practice to be observed in the Matrimonial Office and divorce county courts

7.17. The Lord Chief Justice may with the concurrence of the Lord Chancellor, issue directions for the purpose of securing due observance of statutory requirements and uniformity of practice in matrimonial proceedings in the Matrimonial Office and divorce county courts.

PART VIII

ENFORCEMENT OF ORDERS

Application

8.1. In this Part, unless the context otherwise requires—

"matrimonial order" means an order made in matrimonial proceedings for the periodical payment of money;

"government stock" means any stock issued by Her Majesty's government in the United Kingdom or any funds of or annuity granted by that body;

"judgment creditor" means the person entitled to payments under an order;

"judgment debtor" means the person liable to make payments under an
order.

GARNISHEE PROCEEDINGS

Attachment of debt due to judgment debtor

8.2.—(1) On the application of the judgment creditor where there is an
amount remaining unpaid by the judgment debtor under a matrimonial order
and any other person within the jurisdiction (hereinafter referred to as "the
garnishee") is in debt to the judgment debtor, the court may, subject to the
provisions of paragraph (2) and rules 8.3 to 8.8 and 8.10 and to any other
statutory provision, order the garnishee to pay the judgment creditor the
amount of any debt due or accruing to the judgment debtor from the garnishee,
or so much thereof as is sufficient to satisfy the order and the costs of the
garnishee proceedings.

(2) An order under this rule shall in the first instance be an order to show
cause, specifying the time and place for further consideration of the matter,
and in the meantime attaching such debt as is mentioned in paragraph (1), or
so much thereof as may be specified in the order, to answer the order
mentioned in that paragraph and the costs of the garnishee proceedings.

(3) In this rule "the garnishee" shall include a limited company having a
place of business within the jurisdiction or a firm any member of which is
resident within the jurisdiction and a garnishee order may be made against
any firm in the name of the firm; and any appearance by any member then
within the jurisdiction pursuant to an order made under this rule shall be a
sufficient appearance by the firm.

Application for order

8.3. An application for an order under rule 8.2 must be made ex parte
supported by an affidavit—

(*a*) identifying the order to be enforced and stating the amount remaining
unpaid under it at the time of the application;

(*b*) stating that to the best of the information and belief of the deponent
the garnishee (naming him) is within the jurisdiction and is indebted
to the judgment debtor and stating the sources of the deponent's
information and the grounds for his belief; and

(*c*) stating, where the garnishee is a bank having more than one place of
business, the name and address of the branch at which the judgment
debtor's account is believed to be held or, if it be the case, that this
information is not known to the deponent.

Service and effect of order to show cause

8.4.—(1) An order under rule 8.12 to show cause must, at least 7 days
before the time appointed thereby for the further consideration of the matter,
be served—

(*a*) on the garnishee personally, and

(*b*) unless the court otherwise directs, on the judgment debtor.

(2) Such an order shall bind in the hands of the garnishee as from the service of the order on him any debt specified in the order or so much thereof as may be so specified.

No appearance or dispute of liability by garnishee

8.5.—(1) Where on the further consideration of the matter the garnishee does not attend or does not dispute the debt due or claimed to be due from him to the judgment debtor, the court may, subject to rule 8.8 make an order absolute under rule 8.2 against the garnishee.

(2) An order absolute under rule 8.2 against the garnishee may be enforced as if judgment for the amount payable thereunder had been given against the garnishee.

Dispute of liability by garnishee

8.6. Where on the further consideration of the matter the garnishee disputes liability to pay the debt due or claimed to be due from him to the judgment debtor, the court may summarily determine the question at issue or order that any question necessary for determining the liability of the garnishee be tried in any manner in which any question or issue in an action may be tried.

Claims of third persons

8.7.—(1) If in garnishee proceedings it is brought to the notice of the court that some other person than the judgment debtor is or claims to be entitled to the debt sought to be attached or has or claims to have a charge or lien upon it, the court may order that person to attend before the court and state the nature of his claim with particulars thereof.

(2) After hearing any person who attends before the court in compliance with an order under paragraph (1), the court may summarily determine the questions at issue between the claimants or make such other order as it thinks just, including an order that any question or issue necessary for determining the validity of the claim of such other person as is mentioned in paragraph (1) be tried in such manner as is mentioned in rule 8.6.

Discharge of garnishee

8.8. Any payment made by a garnishee in compliance with an order absolute under these Rules, shall be a valid discharge of his liability to the judgment debtor to the extent of the amount paid notwithstanding that the garnishee proceedings are subsequently set aside or the judgment or order from which they arose is reversed.

Money in court

8.9.—(1) Where money is standing to the credit of the judgment debtor in court, the judgment creditor shall not be entitled to take garnishee proceedings in respect of that money but may apply to the court by summons for an order that the money or so much thereof as is sufficient to satisfy the order sought to be enforced and the costs of the application be paid to the judgment creditor.

(2) On issuing a summons under this rule the applicant must produce the summons at the Court Funds Office and leave a copy at that office, and the money to which the application relates shall not be paid out of court until after the determination of the application.

If the application is dismissed, the applicant must give notice of that fact to the Court Funds Office.

(3) Unless the court otherwise directs, the summons must be served on the judgment debtor at least 7 days before the day named therein for the hearing.

(4) The court hearing an application under the rule may make such order with respect to the money in court as it thinks just.

Costs

8.10. The costs of any application for an order under rule 8.2 to 8.9 and of any proceedings arising therefrom or incidental thereto, shall, unless the court otherwise directs, be retained by the judgment creditor out of the money recovered by him under the order and in priority to the judgment debt.

CHARGING ORDERS, STOP ORDERS ETC

Order imposing charge on securities

8.11.—(1) The court may for the purpose of enforcing a matrimonial order by order impose on any interest to which the judgment debtor is beneficially entitled in such of the securities to which this rule applies as may be specified in the order a charge for securing payment of the amount due under the order and interest thereon.

(2) Any such order shall in the first instance be an order to show cause, specifying the time and place for further consideration of the matter and imposing the charge until that time in any event.

(3) The securities to which this rule applies are—

(*a*) any Government stock, and any stock of any company registered under the Companies (Northern Ireland) Order 1986(**a**) including any such stock standing in the name of the Accountant General, and

(*b*) any dividend of or interest payable on such stock.

Application for order under rule 8.13

8.12. An application for an order under rule 8.13 must be made ex parte supported by an affidavit—

(*a*) identifying the order to be enforced, stating the amount unpaid under it at the date of the application and showing that the applicant is entitled to enforce the order;

(*b*) specifying the securities on the judgment debtor's interest in which it is sought to impose a charge and stating in whose name they stand;

(a)   S.I. 1986/1032 (N.I. 6)

(*c*) stating that to the best of the information and belief of the deponent the judgment debtor is beneficially entitled to an interest in the securities in question, describing that interest and stating the sources of the deponent's information or the ground for his belief.

Service of notice of order to show cause

8.13.—(1) Unless the court otherwise directs, a copy of the order under rule 8.11 to show cause must, at least 7 days before the time appointed thereby for the further consideration of the matter, be served on the judgment debtor, and, if he does not attend on such consideration, proof of service must be given.

(2) Notice of the making of the order to show cause, with a copy of that order, must as soon as practicable after the making of the order be served—

(*a*) where the order relates to Government stock, on the principal office in Belfast of the Bank of Ireland,

(*b*) where the order relates to other stock, on the company concerned,

(*c*) where the order relates to stock standing in the name of the Accountant General, on the proper officer of the Court Funds Office.

Effect of order to show cause

8.14.—(1) No disposition by the judgment debtor of his interest in any securities to which an order under rule 8.11 to show cause relates which is made after the making of that order shall, so long as that order remains in force, be valid as against the judgment creditor.

(2) Until such order is discharged or made absolute, the Bank of Ireland or, as the case may be, a company shall not permit any transfer of any such stock as is specified in the order or pay to any person any dividend thereof or interest payable thereon, except with the authority of the court.

(3) If, after the notice of the making of such order is served on the Bank of Ireland or a company, the Bank or company permits any transfer or makes any payment prohibited by paragraph (2), it shall be liable to pay the judgment creditor the value of the stock transferred or, as the case may be, the amount of the payment made or, if that value or amount is more than sufficient to satisfy the judgment or order to which such order relates, so much thereof as is sufficient to satisfy it.

Making and effect of charging order absolute

8.15.—(1) On the further consideration of the matter the court shall, unless it appears that there is sufficient cause to the contrary, make the order absolute with or without modifications.

(2) Where on the further consideration of the matter it appears to the court that the order should not be made absolute, it shall discharge the order.

(3) A charge imposed by an order under rule 8.11 made absolute under this rule shall have the same effect, and the judgment creditor in whose favour it is made shall, subject to paragraph (4), have the same remedies for enforcing it, as if it were a valid charge effectively made by the judgment debtor.

(4) No proceedings to enforce a charge imposed by an order made absolute under this rule shall be taken until after the expiration of 6 months from the date of the order to show cause.

Discharge, etc of charging order

8.16. The court, on the application of the judgment debtor or any other person interested in the securities to which an order under rule 8.11 relates, may at any time whether before or after the order is made absolute, discharge or vary the order on such terms (if any) as to costs as it thinks just.

Money in court: charging order

8.17.—(1) The court may for the purpose of enforcing a matrimonial order by order impose on any interest to which the judgment debtor is beneficially entitled in any money in court identified in the order a charge for securing payment of the amount due under the order and interest thereon.

(2) Any such order shall in the first instance be an order to show cause, specifying the time and place for the further consideration of the matter and imposing the charge until that time in any event.

(3) Rules 8.12 and 8.13 shall, with the necessary modifications, apply in relation to an application for an order under this rule and to the order as they apply in relation to an application for an order under rule 8.11 and to such order.

(4) Notice of the making of an order under this rule to show cause, with a copy of that order, must as soon as practicable after the making of the order, be served on the proper officer of the Court Funds Office.

(5) Rules 8.14(1), 8.15(1) and (2) and 8.16 shall, with the necessary modifications, apply in relation to an order under this rule as they apply in relation to an order under rule 112.

Jurisdiction of Master to grant injunction or appoint receiver to enforce charge

8.18. The Master shall have power to grant an injunction if, and only so far as, it is ancillary or incidental to an order under rule 8.11 or 8.17, and an application for an injunction under this rule may be joined with the application for the order under rule 8.11 or 8.17 to which it relates.

Funds in court: stop order

8.19.—(1) The court, on the application of the judgment creditor may without notice to the applicant make an order prohibiting the transfer, sale, delivery out or payment of, or other dealing with, funds in court or any part thereof or the income thereon in which the judgment debtor has an interest.

(2) An application for an order under this rule must be made by summons in the cause or matter relating to the funds in court.

(3) The summons must be served on every person whose interest may be affected by the order applied for and on the proper officer of the Court Funds Office but shall not be served on any other person.

(4) Without prejudice to the court's powers and discretion as to costs, the court may order the applicant for an order under this rule to pay the costs of any party to the cause or matter relating to the funds in question, or of any person interested in those funds, occasioned by the application.

Securities not in court: stop notice

8.20.—(1) A judgment creditor claiming to be beneficially entitled to an interest in any securities to which rule 8.11 applies, other than securities in court, who wishes to be notified of any proposed transfer or payment of those securities may avail himself of the provisions of this rule.

(2) A person claiming to be so entitled must file in the court office,

(*a*) an affidavit identifying the securities in question and describing his interest therein by reference to the document under which it arises, and

(*b*) a notice in Form M23, signed by the deponent to the affidavit, and annexed to it, addressed to the Bank of Ireland or, as the case may be, the company concerned

and must serve an office copy of the affidavit and a copy of the notice sealed with the seal of the court on the Bank of that company.

(3) There must be indorsed on the affidavit filed under this rule a notice stating the address to which any such notice as is referred to in rule 8.21(1) is to be sent and, subject to paragraph (4), that address shall for the purpose of that rule be the address for service of the person on whose behalf the affidavit is filed.

(4) A person on whose behalf an affidavit under this rule is filed may change his address for service for the purpose of rule 8.21 by serving on the Bank of Ireland or, as the case may be, the company concerned, a notice to that effect, and as from the date of service of such a notice the address stating thereon shall for the purpose of that rule be the address for service of that person.

Effect of stop notice

8.21.—(1) Where a notice under rule 8.20 has been served on the Bank of Ireland or a company, then, so long as the notice is in force, the Bank or company shall not register a transfer of any stock or make a payment of any dividend or interest, being a transfer or payment restrained by the notice, without serving on the person on whose behalf the notice was filed at his address for service a notice informing him of the request for such transfer or payment.

(2) Where the Bank of Ireland or a company receives a request for such a transfer or payment as is mentioned in paragraph (1) made by or on behalf of the holder of the securities to which the notice under rule 8.20 relates, the Bank or company shall not by reason only of that notice refuse to register the transfer or make the payment for longer than 8 days after receipt of the request except under the authority of an order of the court.

Amendment of stop notice

8.22. If any securities are incorrectly described in a notice filed under rule 8.20, the person on whose behalf the notice was filed may file in the Matrimonial Office or county court office an amended notice and serve on the Bank of Ireland or, as the case may be, the company concerned a copy of that notice sealed with the appropriate seal and where he does so the notice under rule 8.20 shall be deemed to have been served on the Bank or company on the day on which the copy of the amended notice was served on it.

Withdrawal, etc of stop notice

8.23.—(1) The person on whose behalf a notice under rule 8.20 was filed may withdraw it by serving a request for its withdrawal on the Bank of Ireland or, as the case may be, the company on whom the notice was served.

(2) Such request must be signed by the person on whose behalf the notice was filed and his signature must be witnessed by a practising solicitor.

(3) The court, on the application of any person claiming to be beneficially entitled to an interest in the securities to which a notice under rule 8.20 relates, may by order discharge the notice.

(4) An application for an order under paragraph (3) must be made by summons, and the summons must be served on the person on whose behalf the notice under rule 8.20 was filed.

RECEIVERS: EQUITABLE EXECUTION

Appointment of receiver by way of equitable execution

8.24. Where an application is made for the appointment of a receiver by way of equitable execution, the court in determining whether it is just or convenient that the appointment should be made shall have regard to the amount claimed by the judgment creditor, to the amount likely to be obtained by the receiver and to the probable costs of his appointment and may direct an inquiry on any of these matters or any other matter before making the appointment.

Master may appoint receiver, etc

8.25. The Master shall have power to make an order for the appointment of a receiver by way of equitable execution and to grant an injunction if, and only so far as, the injunction is ancillary or incidental to such an order.

Application of rules as to appointment of receiver, etc

8.26. An application for the appointment of a receiver by way of equitable execution shall be made by summons.

Attachment of earnings

8.27. Articles 73 to 79 of the Judgments Enforcement (Northern Ireland) Order 1981 and R.S.C. Order 105 (which deals with attachment of earnings) shall apply to the enforcement of orders made in matrimonial proceedings in a county court as if they were orders of the High Court.

83

Examination as to debts owing to judgment debtor, etc

8.28.—(1) Any party entitled to enforce an order made in matrimonial proceedings may issue and serve a summons on the judgment debtor liable under such order requiring him to attend before the court to be orally examined as to whether any and what debts are owing to the judgment debtor, and whether the judgment debtor has any and what other property or means of satisfying the order.

(2) The summons under paragraph (1) shall be in Form M24 or as near thereto as the circumstances of the case may render necessary and shall be served on the judgment debtor by recorded delivery or personally.

(3) If the judgment debtor shall fail to attend in pursuance of the summons the court may make an order for the attendance of the judgment debtor or any other person and for the production of any books or documents.

(4) An order for attendance under paragraph (3) shall be served personally on such person or persons and within such time as the court shall direct.

(5) Upon the examination the court may make any of the following orders:—

(*a*) a conditional order of garnishee,

(*b*) a charging order or stop order or any order ancillary thereto,

(*c*) an order for the appointment of a receiver by way of equitable execution, under the preceding rules,

(*d*) an attachment of earnings order under Article 73 of the Judgments Enforcement (Northern Ireland) Order 1981.

(6) The evidence given on the examination shall be taken down in writing, not ordinarily by question and answer, but so as to represent as nearly as may be the statement of the examinee. A copy of the note of such evidence shall, on payment of the appropriate fee, be made available to the parties to any such examination, but save as aforesaid no person shall, without leave of the court, be entitled to examine such note or obtain a copy thereof.

JUDGMENT SUMMONSES

Application for issue of judgment summons

8.29.—(1) In this rule and in rules 8.30 and 8.31 unless the context otherwise requires—

"the Order" means the Judgments (Enforcement) (Northern Ireland) Order 1981(**a**),

"order" means an order made in matrimonial proceedings for the periodical payment of money or an order made by the Enforcement of Judgments Office for the payment by instalments of the amount

(**a**) S.I. 1981/226 (N.I. 6)

due under an order made in matrimonial proceedings for payment of a lump sum or costs;

"judgment creditor" means a person entitled to enforce an order;

"debtor" means a person liable under an order;

"judgment summons" means a summons issued under Article 108 of the Order.

(2) An application for the issue of a judgment summons may be made—

(a) in the case of an order of the High Court, to the Matrimonial Office;

(b) in the case of an order of a county court to that court;

by filing an affidavit verifying the amount due under the order and showing how the amount is arrived at.

(3) A judgment summons shall not be issued without the leave of the judge if the debtor is in default under an order of committal made on a previous judgment summons in respect of the same order.

(4) Every judgment summons shall be in Form M25 and shall be served on the debtor personally not less than 10 clear days before the hearing and at the time of service there shall be paid or tendered to the debtor a sum reasonably sufficient to cover his expenses in travelling to and from the court.

(5) Where a judgment summons has not been served in due time, it may by leave of the registrar be reissued and, if necessary, amended from time to time within 6 months of the date of the original judgment summons.

(6) If the judge makes an order for committal, he may direct its execution to be stayed on terms that the debtor pays to the judgment creditor the amount due, together with the costs of the judgment summons, either at a specified time or by instalments, in addition to any sums accruing due under the original order.

(7) All payments under an order made under or an order of committal shall be made to the judgment creditor unless the judge otherwise directs.

(8) Where an order of committal is stayed on such terms as are mentioned in paragraph (9)—

(a) all payments thereafter made shall be deemed to be made, first, in or towards the discharge of any sums from time to time accruing due under the original order and, secondly, in or towards the discharge of the debt in respect of which the judgment summons was issued and the costs of the summons; and

(b) the said order shall not be issued until the judgment creditor has filed an affidavit of default on the part of the debtor.

(9) Where an order of committal has been made but execution of the order is stayed and the debtor subsequently desires to apply for a further stay, he shall attend at or write to the Matrimonial Office or the county court office, as the case may be, and apply for the stay he requires, stating the reasons for his inability to comply with the order, and the Master or chief clerk, as the case may be, shall fix a day for the hearing of the application by the judge and serve notice thereof on the judgment creditor and on the debtor by recorded delivery at least 3 clear days before the day fixed for the hearing.

(10) The judgment creditor shall serve notice by recorded delivery on the debtor of the terms of any order made under this rule whether or not the debtor has attended the hearing.

(11) An order for committal shall be directed to any police officer or other person as the court may direct for execution.

Further provisions as to judgment summonses

8.30.—(1) R.S.C. Order 38, rule 2(3) (which enables evidence to be given by affidavit in certain cases) shall apply to a judgment summons issued in the High Court or a county court as if it were an originating summons.

(2) Witnesses may be summoned to prove the means of the debtor in the same manner as witnesses are summoned to give evidence on the hearing of a cause, and writs of subpoena or witness summonses may be issued for that purpose.

(3) Where the debtor appears at the hearing, the travelling expenses paid to him may, if the judge so directs, be allowed as expenses of a witness, but if the debtor appears at the hearing and no order of commitment is made, the judge may allow to the debtor, by way of set-off or otherwise, his proper costs, including compensation for loss of time, as upon an attendance by a defendant at a trial in court.

Special provisions as to judgment summonses in divorce county courts

8.31. C.C.R. Order 40 (which deals with enforcement of decrees) shall not apply to a judgment summons issued in a county court.

Removal of divorce county court order into High Court

8.32.—(1) Any order made by a county court in matrimonial proceedings may, on an application made to the High Court ex parte by affidavit by the person entitled to enforce the order, be removed into the High Court by direction of the Master, if he is satisfied that the order cannot conveniently be enforced in the county court.

Brian Hutton
John MacDermott
Malachy J. Higgins
J. F. B. Russell
F. Brian Hall
Mary Connolly

Dated 19th July 1996.

I concur   *Mackay of Clashfern, C.*

Dated 25th July 1996.

FORM M1

ORIGINATING SUMMONS

In the High Court of Justice in Northern Ireland

Family Division[1]

In the County Court for the Division of[1]

In the Matter of a Proposed Petition by AB for the annulment of his (or her) Marriage with CB.

LET   of   in the County of   attend the Judge in Chambers at   on the   day of   19   , at   o'clock in the   noon on the hearing of an application of   for an order that the said   may be at liberty to file a petition for the annulment of his (or her) marriage with the said   solemnized on the   day of   19   , notwithstanding that 3 years have passed since the date of the said marriage.

A copy of the affidavit to be used in support of the application is delivered herewith.

If you wish to be heard on the application, you must attend at the time and place above mentioned and if you do not attend, such order will be made and proceedings taken as the Judge may think just and expedient.

Dated this   day of   19   .

THIS SUMMONS was taken out by   solicitor for the above-named.

Note:

1. You must complete the accompanying acknowledgement of service and send it so as to reach the court within fourteen days after you receive this summons.

2. In default of your giving notice of intention to defend the court will proceed to hear and determine the application and make such order thereon as it may think fit, notwithstanding your absence.

3. If you intend to instruct a solicitor to act for you, you should at once give him all the documents served on you, so that he may take the necessary steps on your behalf.

(1) Delete if inapplicable

FORM M2

HEADING OF PETITION

In the High Court of Justice in Northern Ireland

Family Division[1]

In the County Court for the Division of[1]

The Petition of AB—

    1.

    2.

    3.

Etc

(1) Delete if inapplicable

GENERAL HEARING OF PROCEEDINGS

In the High Court of Justice in Northern Ireland

Family Division[1]

In the County Court for the Division of[1]

Between	Petitioner
and	Respondent
and	Co-Respondent[1]

(1) Delete if inapplicable

STATEMENT OF ARRANGEMENTS FOR CHILDR

In the High Court of Justice in Northern Ireland

Family Division[1]

In the County Court for the Division of[1]

Between   Petitione₁

and   Respondent

and   Co-Respondent[1]

To the Petitioner

You must complete this form
if you or the respondent have any children ● under 16
                          or ● over 16 but under 18 if they are
at school or college or are
training for a trade, profession
or vocation.

Please use black ink.

Please complete Parts I, II and III.

Before you issue a petition for divorce try to reach agreement with your husband/wife over the proposals for the children's future. There is space for him/her to sign at the end of this form if agreement is reached.

If your husband/wife does not agree with the proposals he/she will have the opportunity at a later stage to state why he/she does not agree and will be able to make his/her own proposals.

You should take or send the completed form, signed by you (and, if agreement is reached, by your husband/wife) together with a copy to the court when you issue your petition.

If you wish to apply for any of the orders which may be available to you under Part II or III of the Children (Northern Ireland) Order 1995 you are advised to see a solicitor.

The court will only make an order if it considers that an order will be better for the child(ren) than no order.

You should obtain legal advice from a solicitor or, alternatively, from an advice agency. Addresses of solicitors and advice agencies can be obtained from the Yellow Pages.

To the Respondent

The petitioner has completed Part I, II and III of this form which will be sent to the court at the same time that the divorce petition is filed.

Please read all parts of the form carefully.

If you agree with the arrangements and proposals for the children you should sign Part IV of the form.

Please use black ink. You should return the form to the petitioner, or his/her solicitor.

If you do not agree with all or some of the arrangements or proposals you will be given the opportunity of saying so when the divorce petition is served on you.

Part I — Details of the children

Please read the instructions for boxes 1, 2 and 3 before you complete this section

1. Children of both parties *(Give details only of any children born to you and the Respondent or adopted by you both)*

Forenames	Surname	Date of Birth
(i)		
(ii)		
(iii)		
(iv)		
(v)		

2. Other children of the family *(Give details of any children treated by both of you as children of the family: for example your own or the Respondent's)*

Forenames	Surname	Date of Birth	Relationship to Yourself	Respondent
(i)				
(ii)				
(iii)				
(iv)				
(v)				

3. Other children who are not children of the family *(Give details of any children born to you or the Respondent that have not been treated as children of the family, or adopted by you both)*

Forenames	Surname	Date of Birth
(i)		
(ii)		
(iii)		
(iv)		
(v)		

Part II — Arrangements for the children of the family

This part of the form must be completed. Give details for each child if arrangements are different. If necessary, continue on another sheet and attach it to this form

4. Home details *(please tick the appropriate boxes)*

(a) The address at which the children now live	
(b) Give details of the number of living rooms, bedrooms, etc at the address in (a)	
(c) Is the house rented or owned and by whom? Is the rent or any mortgage being regularly paid?	☐ No ☐ Yes
(d) Give the names of all other persons living with the children including your husband/wife if he/she lives there. State their relationship to the children.	
(e) Will there be any change in these arrangements?	☐ No ☐ Yes *(please give details)*

92

5. Education and training details *(please tick the appropriate boxes)*

(a) Give the names of the school, college or place of training attended by each child.	
(b) Do the children have any special educational needs?	☐ No ☐ Yes *(please give details)*
(c) Is the school, college or place of training, fee-paying? Are fees being regularly paid?	☐ No ☐ Yes *(please give details of how much the fees are per term/year)* ☐ No ☐ Yes *(please give details)*
(d) Will there be any change in these arrangements?	☐ No ☐ Yes *(please give details)*

6. Childcare details *(please tick the appropriate boxes)*

(a) Which parent looks after the children from day to day? If responsibility is shared, please give details.	
(b) Does that parent go out to work?	☐ No ☐ Yes *(please give details of his/her hours of work)*
(c) Does someone look after the children when the parent is not there?	☐ No ☐ Yes *(please give details)*
(d) Who looks after the children during school holidays?	
(e) Will there be any change in these arrangements?	☐ No ☐ Yes *(please give details)*

7. Maintenance *(please tick the appropriate boxes)*

(a) Does your husband/wife pay towards the upkeep of the children? If there is another source of maintenance please specify.	☐ No ☐ Yes	*(please give details of how much)*
(b) Is the payment made under a court order?	☐ No ☐ Yes	*(please give details)*
(c) Is the payment made following an assessment by the Child Support Agency?	☐ No ☐ Yes	
(d) Has maintenance for the children been agreed?	☐ No ☐ Yes	
If not, will you be applying for a maintenance order from the court?	☐ No ☐ Yes	*(please give details)*
Child support maintenance through the Child Support Agency.	☐ No ☐ Yes	

8. Details for contact with the children *(please tick the appropriate boxes)*

(a) Do the children see your husband/wife?	☐ No ☐ Yes	*(please give details of how often and where)*
(b) Do the children ever stay with your husband/wife?	☐ No ☐ Yes	*(please give details of how much)*
(c) Will there be any change to these arrangements?	☐ No ☐ Yes	*(please give details of how much)*

9. Details of health   *(please tick the appropriate boxes)*

(*a*) Are the children generally in good health?	☐ No	☐ Yes	*(please give details of any serious disability or chronic illness)*
(*b*) Do the children have any special health needs?	☐ No	☐ Yes	*(please give details of the care needed and how it is to be provided)*

10. Details of care and other court proceedings   *(please tick the appropriate boxes)*

(*a*) Are the children in the care of a local authority, or under the supervision of a social worker or probation officer?	☐ No	☐ Yes	*(please give details including any court proceedings)*
(*b*) Are any of the children on the Child Protection Register?	☐ No	☐ Yes	*(please give details of the local authority and the date of registration)*
(*c*) Are there or have there been any proceedings in any court involving the children, for example adoption, custody/ residence, access/contact wardship, care, supervision or maintenance (you need not include any Child Support Agency proceedings)?	☐ No	☐ Yes	*(please give details and send a copy of any order to the court)*

95

Part III — To the Petitioner

Conciliation

If you and your husband/wife do not agree about the arrangements for the child(ren), would you agree to discuss the matter with a Conciliator and your husband/wife?

☐ No   ☐ Yes

Declaration

I declare that the information I have given is correct and complete to the best of my knowledge.

Signed: . . . . (Petitioner)

Date: . . . .

Part IV — To the Respondent

I agree with the arrangements and proposals contained in Part I and II of this form.

Signed: . . . . (Respondent)

Date: . . . .

NOTICE OF PROCEEDINGS

[Heading as in Form M3]

TAKE NOTICE that a petition for divorce (originating summons)[1] has been presented to the court. A sealed copy of it [and a copy of the petitioner's statement of arrangements regarding the children] [is] [are] delivered with this notice.

1. You must complete and detach the acknowledgement of service in Form M6 and send it so as to reach the Matrimonial Office, Royal Courts of Justice, Chichester Street, Belfast, within 14 days after you receive this notice, inclusive of the day of receipt. Delay in returning the form may add to the costs.

2. If you intend to instruct a solicitor to act for you, you should at once give him all documents which have been served on you, so that he may send the acknowledgement to the Matrimonial Office on your behalf. If you do not intend to instruct a solicitor, you should nevertheless give an address for service in the acknowledgement so that any documents affecting your interests which are sent to you will in fact reach you. Any change of address should be notified to the Matrimonial Office.

NOTES ON QUESTIONS IN FORM M6

3. If you answer Yes to Question [4 or 7][1] you must within 35 days after you receive this notice, inclusive of the day of receipt, file in the Matrimonial Office, Royal Courts of Justice, Chichester Street, Belfast, an answer to the petition, and deliver a copy to every other party to the proceedings. The case will then be transferred to the High Court[2].

4.[1] Before you answer Yes to Question 5 you should understand that—

(*a*) you are under no obligation to answer this question but you may do so if you wish;

(*b*) the answer Yes will be treated by the court as an admission on which the petitioner is entitled to rely and may result in an order for costs being made against you;

(*c*) if you are in any doubt about the answer to give you should consult a solicitor.

5.[1] Before you answer Yes to Question 6 you should understand that—

(*a*) if the petitioner satisfies the court that the petitioner and you have lived apart for 2 years immediately before the presentation of the petition and that you consent to a decree, the court will grant one unless it considers that the marriage has not broken down irretrievably;

(*b*) a decree absolute of divorce will end your marriage so that—

(i) any right you may have to a pension which depends on the marriage continuing will be affected;

(ii) you will not be able to claim a State widow's pension when the petitioner dies;

(*c*) once the court grants a decree absolute of divorce or a decree of judicial separation, you will lose your right to inherit from the petitioner if he or she dies without having made a will;

(*d*) a decree may have other consequences in your case depending on your particular circumstances and if you are in any doubt about these you would be well advised to consult a solicitor.

6.[(1)] If after consenting you wish to withdraw your consent you must immediately inform the Matrimonial Office and give notice to the petitioner.

7.[(1)] The petitioner relies in support of the petition on the fact that the parties to the marriage have lived apart for at least 5 years. Article 12 of the Matrimonial Causes (Northern Ireland) Order 1978 provides that if in such a case the respondent applies to the court for it to consider the respondent's financial position after the divorce, a decree nisi based on 5 years' separation only cannot be made absolute unless the court is satisfied that the petitioner has made or will make proper financial provision for the respondent, or else that the petitioner should not be required to make any financial provision for the respondent. The petition will tell you whether the petitioner proposes to make any financial provision for you. It is important that you should consider this information carefully before answering Question 7 in the acknowledgement.

8.[(1)] If you answer Yes to Question 8 you must, before the decree is made absolute, make application to the court by filing and serving on the petitioner a notice in Form M14.

9.[(1)] (*a*) If you do not wish to defend the case but object to the claim for costs, you should answer Yes to Question 9 in the acknowledgement. You must state the grounds on which you object. An objection cannot be entertained unless grounds are given which, if established, would form a valid reason for not paying the costs. If such grounds are given, you will be notified of a date on which you must attend before the judge if you wish to pursue your objection.

(*b*) If you do not object to the claim for costs but simply wish to be heard on the amount to be allowed, you should answer No to Question 9.

(*c*) If you are ordered to pay costs, the amount will, unless agreed between the petitioner and yourself, be fixed by the court, or will be taxed by the taxing master, after lodgment of the petitioner's bill of costs. In the latter event, you will be sent a copy of the bill and will have the right to be heard about the amount before it is finally settled.

10. Please answer Question 10. If your answer to Question 10(*b*) is Yes make sure you sign the form at the end.

11. If you wish to make an application for
— a residence order
— a contact order
— a specific issue order
— a prohibited steps order

in respect of a child you will have to make a separate application on Form C1. Before you apply for any of these orders or any other order which may be available to you under the Children (Northern Ireland) Order 1995 you are advised to see a solicitor.

12. If you wish to contest the petitioner's financial or property claim, you will have an opportunity of doing so when you receive a notice stating that the petitioner intends to proceed with the claim. You will then be required to file an affidavit giving particulars of your property and income and be notified of the date when the claim is to be heard.

13. If you wish to make some financial or property claim on your own account, you will have to make a separate application. If you are in doubt as to the consequences of divorce on your financial position, you should obtain legal advice from a solicitor.

Dated this   day of   19   .

Master

To

(1) Delete if inapplicable
(2) Delete if petition has been presented to the High Court or if the case has already been transferred to the High Court

ACKNOWLEDGEMENT OF SERVICE

If you intend to instruct a solicitor to act for you, give him this form immediately

[Heading as in Form 3]

Read carefully the Notice of Proceedings before answering the following questions.

1. Have you received the originating summons [and copy of the supporting affidavit] [*or* the petition for [divorce]](1) delivered with this form?

2. On what date and at what address did you receive it?

3. Are you the person named as Respondent?

4. Do you intend to defend the case?

*5.(1) [In the case of a petition alleging adultery] Do you admit the adultery alleged in the petition?

*6.(1) [In the case of a petition alleging 2 years' separation coupled with the respondent's consent to a decree being granted]. Do you consent to a decree being granted?

7.(3) [In the case of a petition asking for divorce alleging 5 years' separation]. Do you intend to oppose the grant of a decree on the ground that the divorce will result in grave financial or other hardship to you and that in all the circumstances it would be wrong to dissolve the marriage?

8.(3) In the event of a decree nisi being granted on the basis of 2 years' separation, coupled with the respondent's consent, or 5 years' separation, do you intend to apply to the court for it to consider your financial position as it will be after the divorce?

9.(3) Even if you do not intend to defend the case, do you object to paying the costs of the proceedings? If so, on what grounds?

10. (*a*) Have you received a copy of the Statement of Arrangements for Child[ren].

　　(*b*) Do you agree with the proposals in that Statement of Arrangements? *If not* you may file a written statement of your own views on the present and proposed arrangements for the children. It would help if you sent that statement to the court office with this form.

11. [In the case of proceedings relating to a polygamous marriage]. If you have any wife [or husband] in addition to the petitioner [or applicant] who is not mentioned in the petition [or originating summons], what is the name and address of each such wife [or husband] and the date and place of your marriage to her [or him]?

Dated this   day of   19 .

Signed

Address for service [unless you intend to instruct a solicitor, give your place of residence, or if you do not reside in Northern Ireland, the address of a place to which documents may be sent to you. If you subsequently wish to change your address for service, you must notify the Matrimonial Office, Royal Courts of Justice, Chichester Street, Belfast].

[I am [We are] acting for the Respondent [or the above-named   in this matter].

Signed

Address for service:

AFFIDAVIT OF SERVICE

[Heading as in Form M3]

I,   of   make
Oath and say:

    1. That a sealed copy of the[1]
bearing date the   day of   19   filed in this court was duly served by
me on the said   at   on the   day
of   19   by delivery to the said   personally a sealed copy
thereof [together with copies of the notices in Forms 5 and 6] [Means of knowledge
of identity of the person served must be inserted here].

    Sworn, etc.

([1]) Petition or notice or originating summons.

FORM M8   Rule 2.28(2)

CERTIFICATE OF READINESS

[*Heading as in Form M3*]

To the Master

Sir,

I/We request that you enter this cause for hearing at[1]

I/We certify on the part of the petitioner/respondent (hereinafter called "this party")—

(1) that the requirements of rule 2.28(1) are satisfied;

(2) that there are no pending interlocutory proceedings by or against this party;

(3) that this party does not intend to commence any (further) interlocutory proceedings before trial;

(4) that, so far as concerns this party, the cause is ready for trial.

(Signed)

Solicitor for petitioner/respondent

[1] State, in the case of a petition pending in a divorce county court, the desired place of hearing.

FORM M9   Rule 2.39(1)

NOTICE UNDER RULE 2.39

[Heading as in Form M3]

TAKE NOTICE that the application [state nature of application] which was adjourned on   , has been restored to the list for hearing at   on   o'clock.

(Signed)

Solicitor(s) for the Petitioner/Respondent

To: the Petitioner/Respondent
     the Proper Officer/Chief Clerk

NOTICE OF APPLICATION FOR DECREE NISI TO BE MADE ABSOLUTE

[Heading as in Form M3]

TAKE NOTICE that the petitioner [or respondent] applies for the decree nisi pronounced in his (her) favour on the   day of   19 , to be made absolute.

Dated this   day of   19

Signed
[Solicitor for the] Petitioner
[or Respondent]

CERTIFICATE OF MAKING DECREE NISI ABSOLUTE (DIVORCE)

[Heading as in Form M3]

Referring to the decree made in this cause on the   day of   19 ,
whereby it was decreed that the marriage solemnized on the   day of   19
at   between   the petitioner and   the respondent
be dissolved unless sufficient cause be shown to the court within   from
the making thereof why the said decree should not be made absolute, and no such
cause having been shown it is hereby certified that the said decree was on the   day
of   19 , made final and absolute and that the said marriage was thereby
dissolved.

Dated this   day of   19

Note Divorce effects inheritance under a will

Where a will has already been made by either party to the marriage then, by virtue
of Article 13 of the Wills and Administration Proceedings (Northern Ireland) Order
1994, from the above date on which the decree was made absolute:—

   (*a*) any appointment of the former spouse as an executor or trustee or any
        conferment of a power of appointment on the former spouse takes effect as
        if the former spouse had died on the date on which the marriage is dissolved
        or annulled; and

   (*b*) any property comprising or included in a gift to the former spouse passes as
        if the former spouse had died on that date;

unless a contrary intention appears in the will.

Certificate of Making Decree Nisi Absolute (Nullity)

[Heading as in Form M3]

(Seal)

Referring to the decree made in this cause on the   day of   19 ,
whereby it was ordered that the marriage in fact solemnized on the   day of
         19   at   between   the petitioner and
                              the respondent [in the case of a void marriage
be pronounced and declared to have been by law void and the said petitioner be
pronounced to have been and to be free of all bond of marriage with the said
respondent], [in the case of a voidable marriage be annulled] unless sufficient cause
be shown to the court within   from the making thereof why the said
decree should not be made absolute, and no such cause having been shown, it is
hereby certified that the said decree was on the   day of   19 , made
final and absolute [in the case of a void marriage and that the said marriage was by
law void and that the said petitioner was and is free from all bond of marriage with
the said respondent] [in the case of a voidable marriage and that the said petitioner
was from that date and is free from all bond of marriage with the said respondent].

Dated this   day of   19

NOTICE OF APPLICATION FOR ANCILLARY RELIEF

[Heading as in Form M3]

TAKE NOTICE that the petitioner [or respondent] intends to apply to the court for [here set out the ancillary relief claimed, stating the terms of any agreements as to the order which the court is to be asked to make and, in the case of an application for a property adjustment order or an avoidance of disposition order, stating briefly the nature of the adjustment proposed or the disposition to be set aside. If the application is to vary periodical payments or secured periodical payments for a child state whether there are or have been any proceedings in the Child Support Agency relating to their maintenance].

[If you are applying for any periodical payments or secured periodical payments for a child please state—

whether you are applying for payment—
  — for a step-child;
  — in addition to child support maintenance already payable under a Child Support Agency assessment;
  — to meet expenses arising from a child's disability;
  — to meet expenses incurred by a child being educated or training for work; or
  — on some other ground (please specify)
or that
  — the child or the person with care of the child or the absent parent of the child is not habitually resident in the United Kingdom].

Notice will be given to you of the place and time fixed for the hearing of the application [or the application will be heard by the Master or district judge in chambers at   on   day, the   day of   19 , at   o'clock].

[Unless the parties are agreed upon the terms of the proposed order, and in the case of an application for an order for maintenance pending suit or a financial provision order or variation order:

TAKE NOTICE ALSO that you must file in the [Matrimonial Office, Royal Courts of Justice, Chichester Street, Belfast], [or county court office at   ] within 14 days after you receive this notice, an affidavit giving full particulars of your property and income. You must at the same time send a copy of your affidavit to the [solicitor for] the applicant.

[If you wish to allege that the petitioner [or respondent] has property or income, you should say so in your affidavit].

Dated this   day of   19

                    (Signed)

                    [Solicitor for the] Respondent
                    [or Petitioner]

NOTICE OF APPLICATION UNDER RULE 2.48

[Heading as in Form M3]

TAKE NOTICE that the respondent applies to the court under Article 12(2) of the Matrimonial Causes (Northern Ireland) Order 1978 for the court to consider the financial position of the respondent after the divorce.

The application will be heard on a date to be fixed [or if, in the case of an application made after a decree nisi], a date has been fixed by the Master in chambers at   on   day, the   day of   19 , at   o'clock].

[Unless the petitioner has already filed an affidavit in connection with an application for ancillary relief under rule 2.63(2)].

TAKE NOTICE ALSO that you must within 14 days after you receive this notice, file in the [Matrimonial Office, Royal Courts of Justice, Chichester Street, Belfast], [or county court office at   ] an affidavit giving full particulars of your property and income. You must at the same time send a copy of your affidavit to the [solicitor for the] respondent.

[If you wish to allege that the respondent has property or income, you should say so in your affidavit].

Dated this   day of   19

(Signed)

[Solicitor for the] Respondent

NOTICE OF INTENTION TO PROCEED WITH APPLICATION FOR ANCILLARY RELIEF
MADE IN PETITION OR ANSWER

[Heading as in Form M3]

The petitioner [or respondent] having applied in his [or her] petition [or answer] for [here set out the ancillary relief claimed and intended to be proceeded with, stating the terms of any agreement as to the order which the court is to be asked to make].

[If you are applying for any periodical payments or secured periodical payments for a child please state—

whether you are applying for payment
— for a step-child;
— in addition to child support maintenance already payable under a Child Support Agency assessment;
— to meet expenses arising from a child's disability;
— to meet expenses incurred by a child being educated or training for work; or
— on some other ground (please specify)
or that the child or the person with care of the child or the absent parent of the child is not habitually resident in the United Kingdom].

[Add where applicable] TAKE NOTICE that the application will be heard by the Master or district judge in chambers at   on   day, the   day of   19   , at   o'clock.

TAKE NOTICE [ALSO] that [continue as in fourth paragraph of Form M13].

Dated this   day of   19

(Signed)
[Solicitor for the] Petitioner
[or Respondent]

NOTICE OF ALLEGATION IN PROCEEDINGS FOR ANCILLARY RELIEF

[Heading as in Form M3]

TAKE NOTICE that this affidavit has been filed in proceedings for [state nature of application] and that if you wish to be heard on any matter affecting you in the proceedings you may intervene by applying to the court, within 7 days after you receive this notice, inclusive of the day of receipt, for directions as to the filing and service of pleadings and as to the further conduct of the proceedings.

Dated this   day of   19

Issued by

[Solicitor for the] Petitioner
[or Respondent]

NOTICE OF REQUEST FOR PERIODICAL PAYMENTS ORDER AT SAME RATE AS ORDER
FOR MAINTENANCE PENDING SUIT

[Heading as in Form M3]

To   of   . The petitioner [or
respondent] having on the   day of   19 , obtained an order for payment
by you of maintenance pending suit at the rate of

AND the petitioner [or respondent] having applied to his [her] petition [or answer]
for a periodical payments order for himself [or herself].

TAKE NOTICE that the petitioner [or respondent] has requested the court to
make a periodical payments order for himself [or herself] providing for payments by
you at the same rate as those mentioned above.

AND TAKE NOTICE that if you object to the making of such a periodical
payments order, you must give notice to that effect to the [proper officer] [or chief
clerk] and the petitioner [or respondent] within 14 days after service of this notice
on you, and if you do not do so, the Master may make such a periodical payments
order without further notice to you.

Dated this   day of   19

[Proper Officer]
[Chief Clerk]

ORIGINATING SUMMONS FOR MAINTENANCE

In the High Court of Justice in Northern Ireland

Family Division[1]

In the County Court for the Division of[1]

In the Matter of an Application by AB under Article 29 of the Matrimonial Causes (Northern Ireland) Order 1978.

       AB   Applicant

       CB   Respondent

LET the respondent CB[2] attend before the Judge in Chambers at the Royal Courts of Justice, Chichester Street, Belfast, [or as the case may be] on   day, the   day of   19 , at   o'clock, on the hearing of an application of AB[3] who claims that the said CB, being the lawful husband of the applicant.

     (*a*) has failed to provide reasonable maintenance for the applicant, or

     (*b*) has failed to provide, or to make proper contribution towards, reasonable maintenance for any child of the family,

and applies that the said CB be ordered [here set out the relief claimed].

The applicant further applies that the costs of this application be provided for.

Dated the   day of   19

This summons was taken out by

Solicitors for the Applicant

To CB[4]

TAKE NOTICE that—

1. A copy of the affidavit to be used in support of the application is delivered herewith.

2. You must complete the accompanying acknowledgement of service and send it so as to reach the court within 14 days after you receive this summons.

3. In default of your giving notice of intention to defend the court will proceed to hear and determine the application and make such order thereon as it may think fit, notwithstanding your absence.

4. In the event of your giving notice of intention to defend you are required within 21 days after the time limited for giving such notice to file in the Matrimonial Office [or county court office] at the address above-mentioned an affidavit in answer to the application setting out the grounds on which you intend to contest the application

and setting forth in a schedule to the affidavit full particulars of your property and income. You must at the same time send a copy of your affidavit (with the schedule) to the Solicitor for the Applicant.

5. If you intend to instruct a solicitor to act for you, you should at once give him all the documents served on you, so that he may take the necessary steps on your behalf.

(^{1}) Delete if inapplicable
(^{2}) Name, address and description of respondent
(^{3}) Name and address of applicant
(^{4}) Name, address and description of respondent

NOTICE UNDER RULE 3.1(5)

[Heading as in Form M18]

To

TAKE NOTICE that in proceedings by AB[1] in the High Court of Justice in Northern Ireland [or in the County Court for the Division of   ] under Article 29 of the Matrimonial Causes (Northern Ireland) Order 1978 it has been alleged by CB[2] husband of the said AB, that you have committed adultery with the said AB AND FURTHER TAKE NOTICE that you are at liberty within 14[3] days after service of this notice on you to give notice of intention to defend in the proceedings either in person or by your Solicitor at the Matrimonial Office, Royal Courts of Justice, Chichester Street, Belfast, [or county court office at   ], and to intervene in the proceedings and defend all or any of the charges set forth in the copy affidavit served on you with this notice.

This notice is issued by[4]

Dated the   day of   19

[Proper Officer]
[Chief Clerk]

1. You must complete the accompanying acknowledgement of service and send it so as to reach the Matrimonial Office [or county court office] within 14 days after you receive this summons.

2. In default of your giving notice of intention to defend the court will proceed to hear and determine the application and make such order thereon as it may think fit, notwithstanding your absence.

3. If you intend to instruct a solicitor to act for you, you should at once give him all the documents served on you, so that he may take the necessary steps on your behalf.

[1] State name and address of wife
[2] State name, address and description of husband
[3] Or as the case may be
[4] State name and address of petitioner or solicitor

ORIGINATING SUMMONS FOR ALTERATION OF MAINTENANCE AGREEMENT DURING
THE LIFETIME OF THE PARTIES

In the High Court of Justice in Northern Ireland

Family Division(¹)

In the County Court for the Division of⁽¹⁾

IN THE MATTER of an Application under Article 37 of the Matrimonial Causes
(Northern Ireland) Order 1978

Between   Applicant

and   Respondent

LET   of   attend before the
Judge in Chambers at the Royal Courts of Justice, Chichester Street, Belfast, [or as
the case may be] on   day, the   day of   19 ,
at   o'clock, on the hearing of an application of AB who claims that the
agreement made between the said AB and the said   on the   day
of   19 , should be altered as shown in the affidavit
accompanying this summons so as to [make different] [contain] financial
arrangements.

Dated the   day of   19

This summons was taken out by solicitor for the above-named AB

To

TAKE NOTICE:—

The Notice appended to the Summons should follow the Notice in Form M18 but
the words "in a schedule to the affidavit" in paragraph 4 should be deleted.

(¹) Delete if inapplicable

ORIGINATING SUMMONS FOR ALTERATION OF MAINTENANCE AGREEMENT AFTER
THE DEATH OF ONE OF THE PARTIES

In the High Court of Justice in Northern Ireland

Family Division[1]

In the County Court for the Division of[1]

IN THE MATTER of an Application under Article 38 of the Matrimonial Causes
(Northern Ireland) Order 1978

Between   Applicant

and   Respondent

LET   of   attend before the Judge
in Chambers at the Royal Courts of Justice, Chichester Street, Belfast, [or as the case
may be] on   day, the   day of   19   , at   o'clock, on
the hearing of an application that the agreement made on the   day of   between
[   ] and   who died on   on the   day
of   19   , should be altered as shown in the affidavit accompanying this
summons so as to [make different] [contain] financial arrangements.

Dated the   day of   19

This summons was taken out by solicitor for the above-named

To

TAKE NOTICE:—

The Notice appended to the Summons should follow the Notice in Form M18 but
the words "in a schedule to the affidavit" in paragraph 4 should be deleted.

([1]) Delete if inapplicable

NOTICE TO BE INDORSED ON DOCUMENT SERVED IN ACCORDANCE WITH RULE 6.4

To   of

TAKE NOTICE that the contents or purport of this document are to be communicated to the respondent [or as the case may be], the said   if he is over 16 [*add, if the person to be served is by reason of mental disorder within the meaning of the Mental Health (Northern Ireland) Order 1986 incapable of managing and administering his property and affairs;* unless you are satisfied [after consultation with the responsible medical officer within the meaning of the Mental Health Act (Northern Ireland) Order 1986, or if the said   is not liable to be detained or subject to guardianship under that Order, his medical attendant]* that communication will be detrimental to his mental condition].

* Delete these words if the document is served on the responsible medical officer or medical attendant.

AFFIDAVIT AND NOTICE UNDER RULE 8.20

[Heading as in Form M3]

I, A.B. [or C.D. the solicitor for A.B.] of   make oath
and say that according to the best of my knowledge, information and belief I am [or
the said A.B. is] beneficially entitled under the above-mentioned settlement [or as
may be] to an interest in the securities specified in the notice hereto annexed.

Sworn, etc.

This affidavit is filed on behalf of A.B. whose address is

Notice to be annexed to the affidavit.

To the Governor and Company
of the Bank of Ireland
[or as may be]

TAKE NOTICE that the securities comprised in and subject to the trusts of the
settlement [or as may be] referred to in the affidavit to which this notice is annexed
consist of the following, namely [specify the stock, shares, etc, stating the names in
which it stands].

This notice is intended to stop the transfer of the said securities and not the
payment of any dividend thereof or interest thereon [or and also the payment of any
dividend thereof or interest thereon].

(Signed) A.B. [or C.D. if affidavit sworn by him]

Summons under Rule 8.28

[Heading as in Form M3]

WHEREAS the petitioner obtained an order against the above-named respondent on the   day of   19   , for the sum of £   and there is now due and payable under the said order the sum of £   .

You are therefore hereby SUMMONED to appear personally before the Master in Room   at the Royal Courts of Justice, Chichester Street, Belfast, [or at   ] on   day, the   day of   19   , at   o'clock in the   noon to be examined as to whether any and what debts are owing to you, and whether you have any and what other property or means of satisfying the above-mentioned order.

Dated this   day of   19

To:

[Proper Officer]
[Chief Clerk]

Judgment Summons   (Seal)

[Heading as in Form M3]

WHEREAS the above-named   (hereinafter called "the judgment creditor") obtained an order in this court on the   day of   19 , against   (hereinafter called "the debtor") for [state nature of order].

AND WHEREAS default has been made in payment of the sum of £   payable under the said order and the judgment creditor has required this judgment summons to be issued against you, the said debtor.

YOU ARE HEREBY SUMMONED to appear personally before one of the Judges sitting in this Division at   on the   day of   19 , at   o'clock, to be examined on oath of which you have made default and also to show cause why you should not be committed to prison for such default.

[AND TAKE NOTICE THAT the judgment creditor intends to apply to the court at the hearing of this judgment summons for leave to enforce arrears which became due more than 12 months before the date of this summons].

Dated this   day of   19

£

Amount due and unpaid in respect of order and costs ....
Costs of this summons...
Travelling expenses to be paid to the debtor...
Sum on payment of which this summons will be discharged ....

Note: If payment is made too late to prevent the judgment creditor's attendance on the day of the hearing, you may be liable for further costs.

[The judgment creditor's solicitor is   ].

121

DECLARATION AS TO MARITAL STATUS UNDER ARTICLE 31 OF THE MATRIMONIAL
AND FAMILY PROCEEDINGS (NORTHERN IRELAND) ORDER 1989

In the High Court of Justice in Northern Ireland

Family Division[1]

In the County Court for the Division of[1]

Upon the petition of AB	(the petitioner) and upon
hearing the petitioner and upon hearing CD	(the respondent)

It is declared* that the marriage between   and   was
a valid marriage at its inception, namely the   day of   19 .

Dated

*or, where a declaration is made under Article 31(1)(b) of the 1989 Order, the
following form shall be followed:—

. . . that the marriage between

and   subsisted on the   day of   19 .

*or, where a declaration is made under Article 31(1)(c) of the 1989 Order, the
following form shall be followed:—

. . . that the marriage between

and   did not subsist on the   day of   19 .

*or, where a declaration is made under Article 31(1)(d) of the 1989 Order, the
following form shall be used:—

. . . that the divorce [or annulment or legal separation] in respect of   and
(parties to the marriage) obtained on the   day
of   19 , in   (the country where the divorce, annulment or
legal separation was obtained) is entitled to recognition in Northern Ireland.

*or, where a declaration is made under Article 31(1)(e) of the 1989 Order, the
following form shall be used:—

. . . that the divorce [or annulment or legal separation] in respect of   and
(parties to the marriage) obtained on the   day
of   19 , in   (the country where the divorce, annulment or
legal separation was obtained) is not entitled to recognition in Northern Ireland.

[1] Delete if inapplicable.

EX PARTE ORIGINATING SUMMONS UNDER ARTICLE 17 OF THE MATRIMONIAL AND FAMILY PROCEEDINGS (NORTHERN IRELAND) ORDER 1989

In the High Court of Justice in Northern Ireland

Family Division

In the matter of an application under Article 17 of the Matrimonial and Family Proceedings (Northern Ireland) Order 1989.

LET all parties concerning attend before the Judge in Chambers at the Royal Courts of Justice, Chichester Street, Belfast, on the   day of   19 , at   am/pm on the hearing of an application by   AB that leave be granted to the said   AB   to make an application for an order for financial relief under Part IV of the Matrimonial and Family Proceedings (Northern Ireland) Order 1989.

Dated this   day of   19

This summons was taken out by

of   solicitor for the above-named

applicant whose address is

ORIGINATING SUMMONS UNDER ARTICLE 16 OF THE MATRIMONIAL AND FAMILY PROCEEDINGS (NORTHERN IRELAND) ORDER 1989

In the High Court of Justice in Northern Ireland

Family Division

In the matter of an application under Article 16 of the Matrimonial and Family Proceedings (Northern Ireland) Order 1989.

Between   AB   Applicant

and   CD   Respondent

LET   CD   of
attend before the Judge in Chambers at the Royal Courts of Justice, Chichester Street, Belfast, BT1 3JF, on the   day of   19 , at   am/pm, on the hearing of an application by   AB   for the following relief, namely:

Dated this   day of   19

This summons was taken out by

of   solicitor for the above-named applicant whose address is

ORIGINATING SUMMONS UNDER ARTICLE 28 OF THE MATRIMONIAL AND FAMILY PROCEEDINGS (NORTHERN IRELAND) ORDER 1989

In the High Court of Justice in Northern Ireland

Family Division

In the matter of an application under Article 28 of the Matrimonial and Family Proceedings (Northern Ireland) Order 1989.

Between	AB	Applicant
and	CD	Respondent

LET   CD   of
attend before the Judge in Chambers at the Royal Courts of Justice, Chichester Street, Belfast, BT1 3JF, on the   day of   19   , at   am/pm, on the hearing of an application by   AB   that the court shall make an order restraining   CD   from making any disposition or transferring out of the jurisdiction or otherwise dealing with any property with intent to defeat a claim for financial relief by the applicant under Part IV of the Matrimonial and Family Proceedings (Northern Ireland) Order 1989.

Dated this   day of   19

This summons was taken out by

of   solicitor for the above-named applicant whose address is

NOTICE OF PROCEEDINGS AND ACKNOWLEDGEMENT OF SERVICE

In the High Court of Justice in Northern Ireland

Between   AB   Applicant

and   CD   Respondent

Read carefully this Notice of Proceedings before answering the questions which follow.

NOTICE OF PROCEEDINGS

TAKE NOTICE THAT an application [for financial relief] [to prevent a transaction([1]) has been presented to this court. A sealed copy of it and a copy of the applicant's affidavit in support are delivered with this notice.

1. You must complete and detach the acknowledgement of service and send it so as to reach the court within 31 days after you receive this notice, inclusive of the day of receipt. Delay in returning the form may add to the costs.

2. If you wish to dispute the claim made by the applicant you must file in the court an affidavit in answer within 28 days after the time allowed for sending the acknowledgement of service.

3. If you intend to instruct a solicitor to act for you, you should at once give him all the documents which have been served on you, so that he may send the acknowledgement to the court on your behalf. If you do not intend to instruct a solicitor, you should nevertheless give an address for service in the acknowledgement so that any documents affecting your interests which are sent to you will in fact reach you. This should be your place of residence or, if you do not reside in Northern Ireland, the address of a place in Northern Ireland to which documents may be sent to you. Change of address should be notified to the court.

ACKNOWLEDGEMENT OF SERVICE

In the High Court of Justice in Northern Ireland

Family Division

Between   Applicant

and   Respondent

1. Have you received an originating summons and a copy of the supporting affidavit in respect of the proceedings mentioned above?

2. On what date at what address   Date . . . .
   did you receive them?   Address. . . . .

                                   . . . .

                                   . . . .

                                   . . . .

3. Are you the person named as the respondent in the originating summons?

4. Do you intend to defend the case? If your answer to this question is yes you must follow the instructions in paragraph 2 of the Notice of Proceedings.

5. Even if you do not intend to defend the case do you object to paying the costs of the proceedings and, if so, on what grounds?

Dated this   day of   19

                              Signed. . . . .
                              Respondent

I am [we are] acting for the Respondent in this matter.

                              Signed. . . . .

                              Address for service of documents:

Dated this   day of   19

(^{1}) Or as the case may be

FORM M31   Rule 7.14(1)

NOTICE UNDER RULE 7.13(1)

[Heading as in Form M3]

To

of

These proceedings [include/consist of] an application under the   for
an order that

TAKE NOTICE that it appears that the court would be prevented from making
such an order [in respect of the following children

] because

If you wish to dispute this and to claim that the court should continue to deal with
your application you must say so in writing and send it to the court office within 14
days of having received this notice.

If you do this a date for a hearing will be fixed at which you will be able to say
why you think the court would be able to make the order sought.

The address of the court office is

Dated this   day of   19

[Proper Officer]

[Chief Clerk]

FORM C1

APPLICATION FOR AN ORDER

Children (Northern Ireland) Order 1995

Family Proceedings Rules (Northern Ireland) 1996: Rule 4.5

[In the High Court of Justice in Northern Ireland]

[In the Divorce County Court for the

Division of   ]

[In the Family Care Centre at   ]

1 About you (the applicant)

State • *your title, full name, address, telephone number, date of birth and relationship to each child above*

• *your solicitor's name, address, reference, telephone, FAX and DX numbers.*

2 The child(ren) and the order(s) you are applying for

For each child state • *the full name, date of birth and sex*

• *the type of order(s) you are applying for (for example, residence order, contact order, supervision order, appointment of a guardian).*

3 Other cases which concern the child(ren)

If there have ever been, or there are pending, any court cases which concern

• *a child whose name you have put in paragraph 2*

• *a full, half or step brother or sister of a child whose name you have put in paragraph 2*

• *a person in this case who is or has been, involved in caring for a child whose name you have put in paragraph 2*

attach a copy of the relevant order and give

• *the name of the court*

• *the name and panel address (if known) of the guardian ad litem, if appointed*

• *the name and contact address (if known) of the solicitor appointed for the child(ren).*

4 The respondent(s)

Appendix 3

For each respondent state
- *the title, full name and address*
- *the date of birth (if known) or the age*
- *the relationship to each child.*

5 Others to whom notice is to be given

Appendix 3

For each person state
- *the title, full name and address*
- *the date of birth (if known) or age*
- *the relationship to each child.*

6 The care of the child(ren)

For each child in paragraph 2 state
- *the child's current address and how long the child has lived there*
- *whether it is the child's usual address and who cares for the child there*
- *the child's relationship to the other children (if any).*

7 Social Services

For each child in paragraph 2 state
- *whether the child is known to the Social Services.*
  If so, give the name of the social worker and the address of the relevant Board or Trust.
- *whether the child is, or has been, on the Child Protection Register. If so, give the date of registration.*

8 The education and health of the child(ren)

For each child state
- *the name of the school, college or place of training which the child attends*
- *whether the child is in good health. Give details of any serious disabilities or ill-health*
- *whether the child has any special needs.*

9 The parents of the child(ren)

For each child state
- *the full name of the child's mother and father*
- *whether the parents are, or have been, married to each other*
- *whether the parents live together. If so, where*
- *whether, to your knowledge, either of the parents have been involved in a court case concerning a child. If so, give the date and the name of the court.*

10 The family of the child(ren) (other children)

For any other child not already mentioned in the family (for example, a brother or a half sister) state

- *the full name and address*
- *the date of birth (if known) or age*
- *the relationship of the child to you.*

11 Other adults

State
- *the full name of any other adults (for example, lodgers) who live at the same address as any child named in paragraph 2*
- *whether they live there all the time*
- *whether, to your knowledge the adult has been involved in a court case concerning a child. If so, give the date and the name of the court.*

12 Your reason(s) for applying and any plans for the child(ren)

State briefly your reasons for applying and what you want the court to order

- ***Do not** give a full statement if you are applying for an order under Article 8 of Children (Northern Ireland) Order 1995. You may be asked to provide a full statement later.*
- ***Do not** complete this section if this form is accompanied by a prescribed supplement.*

13 At the court

State
- *whether you will need an interpreter at court (parties are responsible for providing their own). If so, specify the language.*
- *whether disabled facilities will be needed at court.*

Signed   Date

(Applicant)

FORM C2

APPLICATION

- for leave to commence proceedings
  Family Proceedings Rules (Northern Ireland) 1996: Rule 4.4
- for an order or directions in existing family proceedings
  Children (Northern Ireland) Order 1995
- to be joined as, or cease to be, a party in existing family proceedings
  Family Proceedings Rules (Northern Ireland) 1996: Rule 4.8(2)

[In the High Court of Justice in Northern Ireland]

[In the Divorce County Court for the

Division of   ]

[In the Family Care Centre at   ]

The full name(s) of the child(ren)

1 About you (the person making this application)

State • *your title, full name, address, telephone number, date of birth and relationship to each child above*

  • *your solicitor's name, address, reference, telephone, FAX and DX numbers*

  • *if you are already a party to the case, give your description*

     (for example, applicant, respondent or other).

2 The order(s) or direction(s) you are applying for

State for each child • *the full name, date of birth and sex*

  • *the type of order(s) you are applying for (for example, residence order, contact order, supervision order).*

3 Persons to be served with this application

For each respondent to this application state the title, full name and address.

4 Your reason(s) for applying and any plans for the child(ren)

State briefly your reasons for applying.

Do not *give a full statement if you are applying for an order under Article 8 Children (Northern Ireland) Order 1995.*

You may be asked to provide a full statement later.

Signed   Date

(Applicant)

FORM C3

[In the High Court of Justice in Northern Ireland]

[In the Divorce County Court for the

Division of   ]

. [In the Family Care Centre at   ]

NOTICE TO PARTIES OF PROCEEDINGS

[HEARING] [DIRECTIONS APPOINTMENT]

has applied to the court for an order.

The application concerns the following child(ren)

About the [Hearing] [Directions Appointment]

You should attend when the court hears the application at

on

at   [am]   [pm]

The hearing is estimated to last

What to do next

There is a copy of the application with this Notice. You have been named as a party in the application.

Read the application now, and the notes overleaf.

When you go to court please take this Notice with you and show it to a court official.

133

About this Notice

Note 1 **At the hearing or directions appointment**   you will be able to tell the court about any special needs or circumstances of the child(ren).

Note 2 **If Form C4 (Acknowledgement) is enclosed**   you must fill it in and return it to the court as soon as possible, and serve a copy on the other parties.

Note 3 **For legal advice**   go to a solicitor or an advice agency.

Some solicitors specialise in court proceedings which involve children. You can obtain the address of a solicitor or an advice agency from the Yellow Pages or the Law Society.

A solicitor or an advice agency will be able to tell you whether you may be eligible for legal aid.

Note 4 **If you want to apply for an order**   in respect of any of the children named on the Notice, fill in Form C1.

You can obtain the form from a court office. The application must be made to the court sending you this notice.

FORM C3A

[In the High Court of Justice in Northern Ireland]

[In the Divorce County Court for the

Division of   ]

[In the Family Care Centre at   ]

NOTICE TO NON-PARTIES OF PROCEEDINGS

[HEARING] [DIRECTIONS APPOINTMENT]

has applied to the court
for an order.

The application concerns the following child(ren)

About the [Hearing] [Directions Appointment]

The court will hear the application at

on

at   [am]   [pm]

The hearing is estimated to last

What to do next

You have been named in the application. Please read the notes overleaf.

If you go to court please take this Notice with you and show it to a court official.

About this Notice

Note 1   **You do not have the right to take part in the proceedings, at present.**

If you want to take part (become a party to the proceedings) you must apply to the court on Form C2. In all correspondence quote the case number and the child(ren)'s number(s).

You can obtain Form C2 from a court office. The application must be made to the court sending you this notice.

Note 2   For legal advice go to a solicitor or an advice agency.

Some solicitors specialise in court proceedings which involve children. You can obtain the address of a solicitor or an advice agency from the Yellow Pages or the Law Society.

A solicitor or an advice agency will be able to tell you whether you may be eligible for legal aid.

ACKNOWLEDGEMENT

[In the High Court of Justice in Northern Ireland]

[In the Divorce County Court for the
Division of   ]
[In the Family Care Centre at   ]

Date of [Hearing] [Directions Appointment]

What you (the person receiving this form) should do

- Answer the questions overleaf.
- If you need more space for an answer use a separate sheet of paper. Please put your full name, case number and the child(ren)'s number(s) at the top.
- If the applicant has asked the court to order you to make a payment for a child you must also fill in a Statement of Means (Form C7A). You can obtain this form from a court office if one has not been enclosed with the papers served on you.
- When you have answered the questions make copies of both sides of this form. You will need a copy for the applicant, and each party named in Part 4 of Form C1.
- Post, or hand, a copy to the applicant and to each party. Then post, or take, this form, and the Statement of Means if you filled one in, to the court at the address below.

  You must do this **within 14 days** of the date when you were given the Notice of Proceedings, **or** of the postmark on the envelope if the Notice of Proceedings was posted to you.

To be completed by the court

The court office is open

from   am to   pm

on Mondays to Fridays

1 About you	Full name
	Date of birth
	Address
Please give a daytime telephone number if you can.	Telephone Number

137

2 About your solicitor

*If you do not have a solicitor put **None**. (But see note 3 on the Notice of Proceedings which was served on you).*

Name

Address

Telephone Number

FAX Number

DX Number

3 Address to which letters and other papers should be sent.

4 The application was received on:

5 Do you oppose the application?

6 Do you intend to apply to the court for an order?

7 Will you use an interpreter at court?

If Yes state the language into which the interpreter will translate.

Note: If you require an interpreter you must bring your own.

Signed
(Respondent)

Date

FORM C5

CONFIDENTIAL ADDRESS

Family Proceedings Rules (Northern Ireland) 1996: Rule 7.16(2)

The court

The full name(s) of the child(ren)

Your full name

The omitted address

This form is to be used by any party in Family Proceedings who does not wish to reveal the address of their private residence or that of any child. This address will not be revealed to any person save by order of the court. State that address.

FORM C6

STATEMENT OF SERVICE

Family Proceedings Rules (Northern Ireland) 1996: Rule 4.9(5)

[In the High Court of Justice in Northern Ireland]

[In the Divorce County Court for the
Division of   ]

[In the Family Care Centre at   ]

You must	•	give details of service of the application on each of the other parties
	•	give details of service on person to whom notice has to be given
	•	file this form with the court on or before the first Directions Appointment or Hearing of the Proceedings
You should	•	if the person's solicitor was served, give his or her name and address
	•	if the guardian ad litem was served on behalf of the child, give his or her name and **panel** address.
You must indicate	•	the manner, date, time and place of service,
or	•	where service was effected by post, the date, time and place of posting.

Name and address of person served	How, when and where served	Prescribed forms served

I have served the [applicant] [Notice of Proceedings] as stated above.

I am the [applicant] [solicitor for the applicant] [other (state)]

Signed   Date

SUPPLEMENT FOR AN APPLICATION FOR FINANCIAL PROVISION FOR A CHILD OR VARIATION OF FINANCIAL PROVISION FOR A CHILD

Schedule 1 Children (Northern Ireland) Order 1995

[In the High Court of Justice in Northern Ireland]

[In the Divorce County Court for the
Division of   ]

[In the Family Care Centre at   ]

1 About the application

State whether you are seeking

- *an order for a lump sum; a transfer of property; a settlement of property; periodical payments; secured periodical payments*

or - *a variation of an order for periodical payments; secured periodical payments; payment of a lump sum by instalments.*

2 Previous court orders and written agreements

If a written agreement or court order has been made a copy should be attached to this application.

If not available state - *the date*
- *the terms*
- *the parties*
- *the court.*

3 The Child Support Agency

Assessment for maintenance

State whether the Agency has made an assessment ☐ *Yes* ☐ *No*
for the maintenance of the child(ren):

If Yes, state whether you are applying for additional child maintenance

- *because the Child Support Agency will no longer deal with your claim.*
   You should explain why the Agency will not deal with the claim.

or - *on top of payments made through the Child Support Agency.*
   You should explain why you need additional maintenance and confirm that the Child Support Agency's assessment is the maximum amount obtainable.

Written agreement for maintenance

State whether there is a written maintenance agreement: ☐ *Yes* ☐ *No*

If No, state whether you are applying for payment:

☐ for [a] stepchild[ren]

☐ in addition to child support maintenance already paid under a Child Support Agency assessment

☐ to meet expenses arising from the disability of [a] child[ren]

☐ to meet expenses incurred by [a] child[ren] in being educated or training for work

☐ when either the child[ren] OR the person with care of the child[ren] OR the absent parent of the child[ren] is not habitually resident in the United Kingdom

☐ for any other reason *(specify):*

4 About the order

State the terms of the order you ask the court to make and in particular

- *the amount you would like the court to order*
- *whether you would like that amount paid weekly or monthly (if you are not applying for a lump sum)*
- *why you require the payments, or would like the court to carry an existing order.*

5 The collection of payment

If payments are not to be collected and paid to you by the Child Support Agency, give full details of how you would like payments collected. Possible ways are:

☐ **Directly to a bank, building society or post office account**

Give the full name and address, sorting code and the number of the account into which payment is to be made.

☐ **By an attachment of earnings order**

This is a court order which is sent to the employer of the person who is to pay.

☐ **If you would like the court to direct that money is paid in some other way**

Please say what method you would like.

And if you do not mind how the money is paid, please say so. The court will decide how it should be paid.

Signed   Date

(Applicant)

You should now complete a Statement of Means, Form C7A

FORM C7A

STATEMENT OF MEANS

Schedule 1 Children (Northern Ireland) Order 1995

[In the High Court of Justice in Northern Ireland]

[In the Divorce County Court for the
Division of   ]

[In the Family Care Centre at   ]

**Warning   The court will require to see written evidence of unemployment or
sickness; or wage or salary slips, bank statements, and other papers
giving details of your means. This evidence should be attached to this
form or brought with you when you attend the hearing.**

1 About you

State   ● *your title, full name, address, telephone number and date of birth*

●   *whether you are married, single or other*

●   *whether you are the applicant or the respondent.*

2 Your dependants

State for each dependant   ●   *the dependant's title, full name and age*

●   *whether the dependant is a spouse, partner, child
or other*

●   *whether the dependant is wholly or partially
financially dependent on you*

●   *whether the dependant lives with you.*

3 Your employment

State whether you are employed, self-employed or other.

If you are employed, state   ●   *your employment*

●   *your employer's name, address and daytime
telephone number.*

4 Your buildings and land

*List all buildings and land you own, whether in your name alone or jointly, stating
for each*

●   *the address*

●   *the name(s) of the owner(s)*

●   *the current value.*

143

5 Your financial assets

List each bank, building society and post office account, stating for each

- *the name and address where the account is held*
- *the account number*
- *the current balance.*

List all investments and securities (for example, shares, insurance policies) stating for each one the name and quantity and current value.

List all pension schemes, stating for each one the scheme name and the company.

6 Other possessions of value

List all possessions of value (for example, jewellery, antiques, collectable items), stating for each:

- *what they are*
- *the current value.*

7 Your income

	State whether Weekly (W) or Monthly (M)
If employed, state your usual take home pay	£
If self-employed, state	
• your drawings	£
• your gross turnover	£
• your profit after expenses	£
• whether you expect your turnover to increase, decrease or remain the same:	
• the date of the accounts showing the above gross turnover and profit after expenses	Year ending 19
In all cases, state any of the following which you receive	
• Income Support	£
• Child Benefits	£
• Child Support Agency	£
• Other state benefits (specify source)	£
	£
	£
• Pension(s) (specify source)	£
	£
	£
• Contributions from others in the home (total)	£
• Other income (specify source and amount)	£
	£
	£
	£_____
Total income:	£_____

8 Court Orders

Enclose a copy of any order

Court	Case Number	Amount outstanding (£)	Amount of payment (£)	Weekly (W) or Monthly (M)

9 Your expenses

	Amount of payments	Weekly (W) or Monthly (M)	Total debt	Amount of
Mortgage				
1st	————	————	————	————
2nd	————	————	————	————
Rent	————	————		————
Rates	————	————		————
Gas	————	————		————
Electricity	————	————		————
Telephone	————	————		————
Water charges	————	————		————
Credit Card	————	————	————	————
Loans	————	————	————	————
Storecards	————	————	————	
HP Payments	————	————	————	————
TV rental and licence	————	————		————
Mail Order	————	————	————	————
Food	————	————		
Clothing	————	————		
Public transport	————	————		
Car expenses	————	————		
School meals	————	————		
Child minding	————	————		
Maintenance	————	————		————
Child Support Agency	————	————		————
Other payments (give details)	————	————	————	————
	————	————	————	————
	————	————	————	————
Total Payments	————	————	————	————

Signed   Date

[Applicant] [Respondent]

FORM C8

SUPPLEMENT FOR AN APPLICATION FOR
AN EMERGENCY PROTECTION ORDER

Article 63 Children (Northern Ireland) Order 1995

[In the High Court of Justice in Northern Ireland]

[In the Divorce County Court for the
Division of   ]

[In the Family Care Centre at   ]

1 Description of the child(ren)

If a child's identity is not known, state details which will identify the child.
You may enclose a recent photograph of the child, which should be dated.

2 The grounds for the application

The grounds are

ANY   A ☐ that there is reasonable cause to believe that [this]
APPLICANT   [these] child[ren] [is] [are] likely to suffer significant
harm if

             ☐ the child[ren] [is] [are] not removed to
accommodation by or on behalf of this applicant

or ☐ the child[ren] [does] [do] not remain in the place
where [the child] [they] [is] [are] currently being
accommodated.

BOARD OR
TRUST   B ☐ that inquiries are being made about the welfare of the
APPLICANTS   child[ren] under Article 66(1)(*b*) of the Children
(Northern Ireland) Order 1995 **and** those enquiries are
being frustrated by access to the child[ren] being
unreasonably refused to someone who is authorised to
seek access **and** there is reasonable cause to believe that
access to the child[ren] is required as a matter of urgency.

AUTHORISED
PERSON   C ☐ that there is reasonable cause to suspect that the
APPLICANTS   child[ren] [is] [are] suffering, or [is] [are] likely to suffer,
significant harm **and** inquiries are being made with
respect to the welfare of the child[ren] **and** those
inquiries are being frustrated by access to the child[ren]
being unreasonably refused to someone who is authorised
to seek access **and** there is reasonable cause to believe
that access to the child[ren] is required as a matter of
urgency.

147

3 The additional order(s) applied for

☐ information on the whereabouts of the child[ren] (Article 67(1) of the Children (Northern Ireland) Order 1995).

☐ authorisation for entry of premises (Article 67(3) of the Children (Northern Ireland) Order 1995).

☐ authorisation to search for another child on the premises (Article 67(4) of the Children (Northern Ireland) Order 1995).

4 The direction(s) sought

☐ contact (Article 63(6)(*a*) of the Children (Northern Ireland) Order 1995).

☐ a medical or psychiatric examination or other assessment of the child[ren] (Article 63(6)(*b*) of the Children (Northern Ireland) Order 1995).

☐ to be accompanied by a registered medical practitioner, registered nurse or registered health visitor (Article 64(11) of the Children (Northern Ireland) Order 1995)

5 The reason(s) for the application

If you are relying on a report or other documentary evidence, state the date(s) and author(s) and enclose a copy.

Signed   Date

(Applicant)

FORM C9

SUPPLEMENT FOR AN APPLICATION FOR A WARRANT TO ASSIST A PERSON AUTHORISED BY AN EMERGENCY PROTECTION ORDER

Article 67 Children (Northern Ireland) Order 1995

[In the High Court of Justice in Northern Ireland]

[In the Divorce County Court for the
Division of   ]

[In the Family Care Centre at   ]

1 Description of the child(ren)

If a child's identity is not known, state details which will identify the child.
You may enclose a recent photograph of the child, which should be dated.

2 The grounds for the application

An emergency protection order was made on:
(State the date and time, and attach a copy of the order)

and ☐ a person **has been** prevented from exercising powers under the order by being refused entry to premises or access to the child[ren]

or

☐ that a person **is likely to be** prevented from exercising powers under the order by being refused entry to prermises or access to the child[ren]

3 The direction(s) sought

State • *whether you wish to accompany the constable, if the warrant is granted*

• *whether you wish the constable to be accompanied by a registered medical practitioner, registered nurse or registered health visitor, if he so wishes*

• *where the constable is to take the child, if the warrant is executed.*

4 The reason(s) for the application

If you are relying on a report or other documentary evidence, state the date(s) and author(s) and enclose a copy.

Signed   Date
(Applicant)

149

FORM C10

SUPPLEMENT FOR AN APPLICATION FOR A
CARE OR SUPERVISION ORDER

Article 50 Children (Northern Ireland) Order 1995

[In the High Court of Justice in Northern Ireland]

[In the Divorce County Court for the
Division of   ]

[In the Family Care Centre at   ]

---

1 The grounds for the application

The grounds are   that the child[ren] [is] [are] suffering or [is] [are] likely to
suffer, significant harm and the harm, or likelihood of harm,
is attributable to

☐   the care given to the child[ren], or likely to be given
to the child[ren] if the order were not made, not being
what it would be reasonable to expect a parent to give
to the child[ren]

☐   the child[ren] being beyond parental control

2 The reason(s) for the application

*If you are relying on a report or other documentary evidence, state the date(s) and
author(s) and enclose a copy.*

3 Your plans for the child(ren)

Include   ●   *in the case of supervision orders only, any requirements which
you will invite the court to impose pursuant to paragraph 3
Schedule 3 Children (Northern Ireland) Order 1995*

              ●   *in all cases, whether you will invite the court to make an interim
order.*

4 The direction(s) sought

Signed   Date
(Applicant)

SUPPLEMENT FOR AN APPLICATION FOR AUTHORITY TO REFUSE CONTACT WITH A CHILD IN CARE

Article 53(4) Children (Northern Ireland) Order 1995

[In the High Court of Justice in Northern Ireland]

[In the Divorce County Court for the
Division of   ]

[In the Family Care Centre at   ]

1 The current arrangements for contact

State • *the full name(s) of each person who has contact with each child and the current arrangements for contact*

• *whether the Board or Trust has refused contact for 7 days or less.*

2 The order applied for

State the full name and relationship of any person in respect of whom authority to refuse contact with each child is sought.

3 The reason(s) for the application

If you are relying on a report or other documentary evidence state the date(s) and author(s) and enclose a copy.

Signed   Date
(Applicant)

FORM C12

SUPPLEMENT FOR AN APPLICATION FOR CONTACT WITH A CHILD IN CARE

Article 53(2) and (3) Children (Northern Ireland) Order 1995

[In the High Court of Justice in Northern Ireland]

[In the Divorce County Court for the
Division of   ]

[In the Family Care Centre at   ]

1 Your relationship to the child(ren)
State whether
- *you are a parent or guardian*
- *you hold a residence order which was in force immediately before the care order was made*
- *you had care of the child(ren) through an order which was in force immediately before the care order was made.*

2 The order applied for and your reason(s) for the application
If you are relying on a report or other documentary evidence, state the date(s) and author(s) and enclose a copy.

Signed   Date
(Applicant)

FORM C13

SUPPLEMENT FOR AN APPLICATION FOR
A CHILD ASSESSMENT ORDER

Article 62 Children (Northern Ireland) Order 1995

[In the High Court of Justice in Northern Ireland]

[In the Divorce County Court for the
Division of   ]

[In the Family Care Centre at   ]

1 The grounds for the application

The grounds are   that there is reasonable cause to suspect that the child[ren] [is] [are] suffering, or [is] [are] likely to suffer, significant harm

and

an assessment of the state of the child[ren]'s health or development or of the way in which the child[ren] [has] [have] been treated, is required to determine whether or not the child[ren] [is] [are] suffering, or [is] [are] likely to suffer, significant harm

and

it is unlikely that such an assessment will be made, or be satisfactory, in the absence of an order under this section.

State your reason(s) for believing the grounds exist.

If you are relying on a report or other documentary evidence, state the date(s) and author(s) and enclose a copy.

2 The direction(s) sought in respect of the assessment

3 The direction(s) sought in respect of contact

Signed   Date
(Applicant)

FORM C14

SUPPLEMENT FOR AN APPLICATION FOR AN EDUCATION SUPERVISION ORDER

Article 55 Children (Northern Ireland) Order 1995

Paragraph 6 Schedule 4 Children (Northern Ireland) Order 1995

[In the High Court of Justice in Northern Ireland]

[In the Divorce County Court for the
Division of   ]

[In the Family Care Centre at   ]

1 Prior consultation

State the name of the Board or Trust which has been consulted:

☐ The Board or Trust is the authority providing the child[ren] with accommodation or on whose behalf the child[ren] [is] [are] being provided with accommodation.

or

☐ the Board or Trust is the authority within whose area the child[ren] live[s], or will live.

2 The grounds for the application

The ground is that the child[ren] [is] [are] of compulsory school age and [is] [are] not being properly educated.

State your reason(s) for believing the ground exists. If you are relying on a report or other documentary evidence, state the date(s) and author(s) and enclose a copy.

3 The order and direction(s) applied for

Signed   Date
(Applicant)

FORM C14A

SUPPLEMENT FOR AN APPLICATION FOR AN EXTENSION OF
AN EDUCATION SUPERVISION ORDER

Paragraph 5(2) of Schedule 4 to the Children (Northern Ireland) Order 1995

[In the High Court of Justice in Northern Ireland]

[In the Divorce County Court for the
Division of   ]

[In the Family Care Centre at   ]

1 About the Education Supervision Order

State when the order was made and when it is due to end.
Enclose a copy of the order.

2 The extension

State your reason(s) for asking the court to extend the order. If you are relying on
a report or other documentary evidence, state the date(s) and author(s) and enclose
a copy.

Signed   Date
(Applicant)

FORM C15

SUPPLEMENT FOR AN APPLICATION FOR A RECOVERY ORDER

Article 69 Children (Northern Ireland) Order 1995

[In the High Court of Justice in Northern Ireland]

[In the Divorce County Court for the
Division of   ]

[In the Family Care Centre at   ]

1 Particulars of the child(ren)

State whether the child[ren] [is] [are] ☐ in care

or ☐ the subject   *Enclose*
of an   *a copy*
emergency   *of the*
protection   *order*
order

or ☐ in police
protection

If a child's identity is not known, state details that will identify the child.
You may enclose a recent photograph of the child, which should be dated.

2 The order and direction(s) applied for

State
● *whether the child(ren) (is) (are) to be produced to an authorised person specified by the court (Article 69(7) Children (Northern Ireland) Order 1995)*

● *whether you require the court to authorise a constable to enter specified premises (Article 69(3)(d) Children (Northern Ireland) Order 1995).*

3 The grounds for the application

The grounds are that the child[ren] ☐ [has] [have] been unlawfully taken away or [is] [are] being unlawfully kept away from the responsible person

or ☐ [has] [have] run away or [is] [are] staying away from the responsible person

or ☐ [is] [are] missing.

156

4 The reason(s) for the application

Include your ground(s) for believing that the child(ren) (is) (are) on the premises named in paragraph 2 above (if applicable) (Article 69(6) Children (Northern Ireland) Order 1995).

If you are relying on a report or other documentary evidence, state the date(s) and author(s) and enclose a copy.

Signed   Date

(Applicant)

FORM C16

APPLICATION FOR A WARRANT OF ASSISTANCE

Article 178 Children (Northern Ireland) Order 1995

[In the High Court of Justice in Northern Ireland]

[In the Divorce County Court for the
Division of   ]

[In the Family Care Centre at   ]

1 About you (the applicant)

State
- your title, full name, address, telephone number, and relationship to the child(ren) (if any)
- your solicitor's name, address, reference, telephone, FAX and DX numbers
- whether you are:
    - ☐ a person authorised by a Board or Trust
    - ☐ a person authorised by the Department
    - ☐ a supervisor acting under a supervision order

2 Description of the child(ren) (if applicable)

If a child's identity is not known, state details which will identify the child.

You may enclose a recent photograph of the child, which should be dated.

3 The grounds for the application

☐ I am attempting to exercise powers under an enactment within Article 178 of the Children (Northern Ireland) Order 1995 at the following premises (*give full address*):

and

☐ **I have been** prevented from exercising those powers by

☐ **I am likely to be** prevented from exercising those powers by

PERSON
AUTHORISED
BY THE
AUTHORITY

Article 77(5)

☐ [being, or likely to be, refused entry to accommodation provided by a voluntary organisation]

[being, or likely to be, refused access to a child in accommodation provided by a voluntary organisation]

Article 93

☐ [being, or likely to be, refused entry to a a children's home]

[being, or likely to be, refused access to a child in a children's home]

[being, or likely to be, refused access to records kept in a children's home]

Article 108

☐ [being, or likely to be, refused entry to a private foster home]

[being, or likely to be, refused access to a child in a private foster home]

Article 130

☐ [being, or likely to be, refused entry to domestic premises where child-minding is carried on]

[being, or likely to be, refused access to a child on domestic premises where child-minding is carried on]

[being, or likely to be, refused access to records kept in domestic premises where child-minding is carried on]

☐ [being, or likely to be, refused entry to premises on which day care for children under the age of 12 is provided]

[being, or likely to be, refused access to a child in premises on which day care for children under the age of 12 is provided]

[being, or likely, to be refused access to records kept on premises on which day care for children under the age of 12 is provided]

Article 175

☐ [being, or likely to be, refused entry to a residential care, nursing or mental nursing home]

[being, or likely to be, refused access to a child in a residential care, nursing or mental nursing home]

Article 176

☐ [being, or likely to be, refused entry to an independent school]

[being, or likely to be, refused access to a child in an independent school]

	Article 34 Adoption (Northern Ireland) Order 1987	☐ [being, or likely to be, refused entry to premises on which a protected child is, or is likely to be, kept] [being, or likely to be, prevented from visiting a protected child]
		[being, or likely to be, refused entry to any of the premises specified by Article 149]
PERSON AUTHORISSED BY THE DEPARTMENT	*Article 149*	☐ [being, or likely to be, refused access to a child in any of the premises specified by Article 149] [being, or likely to be, refused access to records stored in any of the premises specified in Article 149]
SUPERVISOR UNDER THE SUPERVISION ORDER	*Paragraph 7(1)(b) Schedule 3*	☐ [being, or likely to be, refused entry to accommodation where a supervised child is living]
	Paragraph 7(2)(b) Schedule 3	☐ [being, or likely to be, refused contact with a supervised child by a responsible person]

4 The respondent(s)

For each respondent state the title, full name, address, telephone number and relationship (if any) to each child.

5 The reason(s) for the application

If you are relying on a report or other documentary evidence, state the date(s) and author(s) and enclose a copy.

6 The direction(s) sought

State
- *whether you wish to accompany the constable, if the warrant is granted*
- *whether you wish the constable to be accompanied by a registered medical practitioner, registered nurse or registered health visitor, if he so wishes.*

Signed   Date

(Applicant)

FORM C17

SUPPLEMENT FOR AN APPLICATION FOR AN ORDER TO HOLD A CHILD IN SECURE ACCOMMODATION

Article 44 Children (Northern Ireland) Order 1995

[In the High Court of Justice in Northern Ireland]

[In the Divorce County Court for the
Division of   ]

[In the Family Care Centre at   ]

1 The grounds for the application

The grounds are ☐ that the child[ren] [has] [have] a history of absconding and [is] [are] likely to abscond from any other accommodation and if the child[ren] absconds [he] [she] [they] [is] [are] likely to suffer significant harm.

 ☐ that if the child[ren] [is] [are] kept in any other accommodation, [the child] [they] [is] [are] likely to injure [himself] [herself] [themselves] or other people.

(In the case of a child under the age of 13) ☐ The approval of the Department of Health and Social Services to the placement of the child[ren] in secure accommodation has been granted and is attached.

2 The reason(s) for the application and length of order applied for

If you are relying on a report or other documentary evidence, state the date(s) and author(s) and enclose a copy.

Signed   Date
(Applicant)

161

FORM C18

IN THE MATTER OF THE CHILDREN
(NORTHERN IRELAND) ORDER 1995

and;

Case Number:

The full name(s) of the child(ren)	Date(s) of birth	Child(ren)'s number(s)

[Order]   [Direction]

Ordered by

on

FORM C19

IN THE MATTER OF THE CHILDREN
(NORTHERN IRELAND) ORDER 1995

Record of the Hearing on: Case Number:

The full name(s) of the child(ren)   Child(ren)'s Number(s)

Attendees

Name   Represented by

Evidence

The court read the report/statement of

The court heard oral evidence [on oath] from

Findings

The court made the following findings of fact

Reasons

The reasons for the court's decision are

Dated

IN THE MATTER OF THE CHILDREN
(NORTHERN IRELAND) ORDER 1995

[In the High Court of Justice in Northern Ireland]

[In the Divorce County Court for the
Division of   ]

[In the Family Care Centre at   ]

Order	Emergency Protection Order
	Article 63 Children (Northern Ireland) Order 1995

The full name(s) of the child(ren) Boy or Girl Date(s) of birth

[described as

                                                                      ]

Warning	**It is an offence intentionally to obstruct any person exercising the power under Article 63(4)(b) Children (Northern Ireland) Order 1995 to remove, or prevent the removal, of a child (Article 63(15) Children (Northern Ireland) Order 1995)**

The court grants	an Emergency Protection Order to the applicant who is
	The order gives the applicant parental responsibility for the child[ren].
The court authorises	[the applicant to remove the child[ren] to accommodation provided by or on behalf of the applicant]
	[the applicant to prevent the child[ren] being removed from
	]

[This order directs that any person who can produce the child[ren] to the applicant must do so.]

The court directs that

This order ends on		at	[am]	[pm]
Ordered by				
on		at	[am]	[pm]

About this order	This is an Emergency Protection Order.

About this order This is an Emergency Protection Order.

This order states what has been authorised in respect of the child[ren] and when the order will end.

The court can extend this order for up to 7 days but it can only do this once.

Warning **If you are shown this order, you must comply with it. If you do not, you may commit an offence. Read the order now.**

What you may do You may apply to the court

to **change the directions**

or to **end the order.**

You may apply at any time, but the court will only hear an application to end an order **when 72 hours** have passed since the order was made.

If you would like to ask the court to change the directions, or end the order, you must fill in a form. You can obtain the form from a court office.

If the court has directed that the child[ren] should have a medical, psychiatric or another kind of examination, you may ask the court to allow a doctor of your choice to be at the examination.

What you should do Go to a solicitor as soon as you can.

Some solicitors specialise in court proceedings which involve children. You can obtain the address of a solicitor or an advice agency from the Yellow Pages or the Law Society.

A solicitor or an advice agency will be able to tell you whether you may be eligible for legal aid.

IN THE MATTER OF THE CHILDREN
(NORTHERN IRELAND) ORDER 1995

[In the High Court of Justice in Northern Ireland]

[In the Divorce County Court for the
Division of   ]

[In the Family Care Centre at   ]

Order   [Variation of an Emergency Protection Order direction
          (Article 63(9)(*b*) Children (Northern Ireland) Order 1995)
          [Extension of an Emergency Protection Order
          (Article 64(4) Children (Northern Ireland) Order 1995)
          [Discharge of an Emergency Protection Order
          (Article 64(7) Children (Northern Ireland) Order 1995

          The full name(s) of the child(ren)   Date(s) of birth

The court [extends]
[varies] [discharges]   [[the direction[s] given] [the Emergency Protection Order
                          granted] by [this court] the

                                                                              court]

                          on   at   [am]   [pm]

[The direction(s) are
varied as follows]

[The order now ends on]

          Ordered by

                   on   at   [am]   [pm]

FORM C22

IN THE MATTER OF THE CHILDREN
(NORTHERN IRELAND) ORDER 1995

[In the High Court of Justice in Northern Ireland]

[In the Divorce County Court for the
Division of   ]

[In the Family Care Centre at   ]

Warrant   To assist a person authorised by an Emergency Protection Order
           Article 67(9) Children (Northern Ireland) Order 1995

To all Police Constables

The court was satisfied that

who is the applicant, has been prevented, or is likely to be prevented from exercising powers under an Emergency Protection Order by being refused entry to the named premises or access to the child concerned.

The court authorises

you to assist the applicant to exercise powers under an Emergency Protection Order made on

You may use reasonable force if necessary.

You may assist the applicant
to gain access **to the child**   *Name*

                                       Boy or Girl   *Date of birth*

                                       described as

You may assist the applicant
to gain entry **to the premises**   *known as*

The court directs   [that you should not be accompanied by the person who applied for the warrant]

                                       [that you may, if you wish, be accompanied by

                                           a registered medical practitioner

                                       or   a registered nurse

                                       or   a registered health visitor]

                                       You should execute this warrant in accordance with the orders and directions contained in the Emergency Protection Order.

This warrant has   [not] been made ex parte.

This warrant ends on

Ordered by

on   at   [am]   [pm]

FORM C23

IN THE MATTER OF THE CHILDREN
(NORTHERN IRELAND) ORDER 1995

[In the High Court of Justice in Northern Ireland]

[In the Divorce County Court for the
Division of   ]

[In the Family Care Centre at   ]

Order   Authority to keep a child in Secure Accommodation
             Article 44 Children (Northern Ireland) Order 1995

             The full name(s) of the child   Date of birth

The court authorises

                    to keep the child in secure accommodation until

This order has been made
on the ground that   [the child has a history of absconding and is likely to
                          abscond from any other accommodation, and if the child
                          absconds [he] [she] is likely to suffer significant harm]
                          [if the child is kept in any other accommodation the child
                          is likely to injure [himself] [herself] or other persons]

[The court was satisfied   that the child, not being legally represented, had been
                          informed of [his] [her] right to apply for legal aid and
                          having had the opportunity to apply, had refused or failed
                          to apply]

        Ordered by   _____

                on   _____

169

FORM C24

IN THE MATTER OF THE CHILDREN (NORTHERN IRELAND) ORDER 1995

[In the High Court of Justice in Northern Ireland]

[In the Divorce County Court for the
Division of   ]

[In the Family Care Centre at   ]

Order	Authority to search for another child
	Article 67(4) Children (Northern Ireland) Order 1995

The full name(s) of the child	Boy or Girl	Date of birth

[who is described as]

The court was satisfied that	[an order had been granted on to the applicant for the emergency protection of a child, *known as*
	and that the order had authorised the applicant to enter these premises].
	[there was reasonable cause to believe that the child named in this order may be on those premises and that an Emergency Protection Order ought to be made in respect of that child].

The court authorises	
	who is the applicant
	to enter the premises, *known as*
	and search for the child.

Warning	**It is an offence intentionally to obstruct the applicant from entering or searching the premises specified above (Article 67(4) and (7) Children (Northern Ireland) Order 1989).**

This order has	[not] been made ex parte.

This order ends on	

Ordered by	
on	at [am] [pm]

FORM C25

IN THE MATTER OF THE CHILDREN
(NORTHERN IRELAND) ORDER 1995

[In the High Court of Justice in Northern Ireland]

[In the Divorce County Court for the
Division of   ]

[In the Family Care Centre at   ]

Warrant   To assist a person to gain access to a child or entry to premises
           Article 178 Children (Northern Ireland) Order 1995

To all Police Constables

The court authorises   you to assist

exercise powers under an enactment as specified on
the reverse of this warrant.

You may use reasonable force if necessary.

[You may assist this person
to gain access **to the child**]   *Name*

Boy or Girl   *Date of birth*

described as

[You may assist this person
to gain entry **to the premises**]   *known as*

The court directs   [that you should not be accompanied by the person
who applied for the warrant]

[that you may, if you wish, be accompanied by
        a registered medical practitioner
or   a registered nurse
or   a registered health visitor]

This warrant has   [not] been made ex parte.

Ordered by

on   at   [am]   [pm]

The court is satisfied that the applicant
- ☐ has been prevented from exercising those powers by
- ☐ is likely to be prevented from exercising those powers by

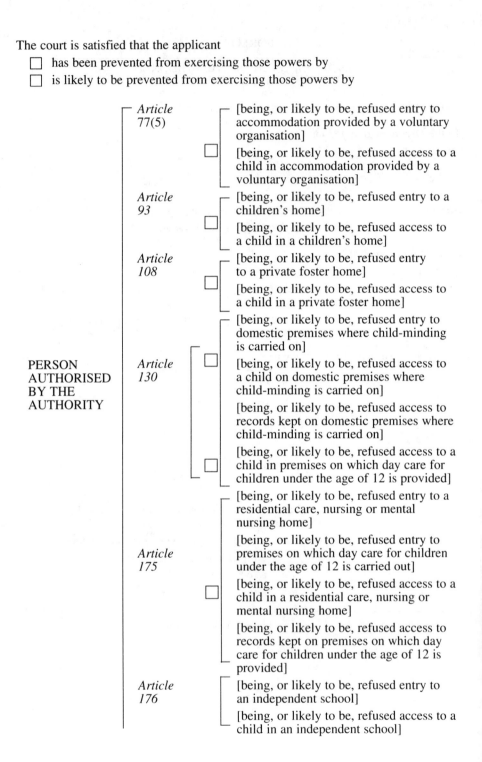

PERSON AUTHORISED BY THE AUTHORITY

Article 77(5)
☐
- [being, or likely to be, refused entry to accommodation provided by a voluntary organisation]
- [being, or likely to be, refused access to a child in accommodation provided by a voluntary organisation]

Article 93
☐
- [being, or likely to be, refused entry to a children's home]
- [being, or likely to be, refused access to a child in a children's home]

Article 108
☐
- [being, or likely to be, refused entry to a private foster home]
- [being, or likely to be, refused access to a child in a private foster home]

Article 130
☐
- [being, or likely to be, refused entry to domestic premises where child-minding is carried on]
- [being, or likely to be, refused access to a child on domestic premises where child-minding is carried on]
- [being, or likely to be, refused access to records kept on domestic premises where child-minding is carried on]
☐
- [being, or likely to be, refused access to a child in premises on which day care for children under the age of 12 is provided]

Article 175
☐
- [being, or likely to be, refused entry to a residential care, nursing or mental nursing home]
- [being, or likely to be, refused entry to premises on which day care for children under the age of 12 is carried out]
- [being, or likely to be, refused access to a child in a residential care, nursing or mental nursing home]
- [being, or likely to be, refused access to records kept on premises on which day care for children under the age of 12 is provided]

Article 176
- [being, or likely to be, refused entry to an independent school]
- [being, or likely to be, refused access to a child in an independent school]

PERSON AUTHORISED BY THE DEPARTMENT	*Article 149*	[being, or likely to be, refused entry to any of the premises specified by Article 149] ☐ [being, or likely to be, refused access to a child in any of the premises specified by Article 149]
	Article 34 Adoption (Northern Ireland) Order 1987	[being, or likely to be, refused entry to premises on which a protected child is, or is likely to be, kept] ☐ [being, or likely to be, refused access to a protected child]
	Paragraph 7(1)(b) Schedule 3	☐ [being, or likely to be, refused entry to accommodation where a supervised child is living]
SUPERVISOR UNDER THE SUPERVISION ORDER	*Paragraph 7(2)(b) Schedule 3*	☐ [being, or likely to be, refused contact with a supervised child by a responsible person]

IN THE MATTER OF THE CHILDREN
(NORTHERN IRELAND) ORDER 1995

[In the High Court of Justice in Northern Ireland]

[In the Divorce County Court for the
Division of   ]

[In the Family Care Centre at   ]

| Order | Recovery of a child |
| | Article 69 Children (Northern Ireland) Order 1995 |

The full name(s) of the child	Boy or Girl	Date of birth

The court is satisfied that	[has parental responsibility for the child by virtue of a [Care Order] [Emergency Protection Order] made on]
	[the child is in police protection and the designated officer is
	]

[The court authorises	
	[a police constable] to remove the child.]
Warning	**It is an offence intentionally to obstruct the person from removing the child**
	(Article 69(9) Children (Northern Ireland) Order 1995)
[The court authorises	[a police constable to enter the premises, *known as*
	and search for the child, using reasonable force if necessary.]
[The court requires	any person who has information about where the child is, or may be, to give that information to a police constable **or** an officer of the court, if asked to do so.]
[The court directs	any person who can produce the child when asked to by
	[a police constable] to do so.]
This order has	[not] been made ex parte.
Ordered by	
on	

IN THE MATTER OF THE CHILDREN
(NORTHERN IRELAND) ORDER 1995

[In the High Court of Justice in Northern Ireland]

[In the Divorce County Court for the
Division of   ]

[In the Family Care Centre at   ]

Order	[Care Order
	Article 50 Children (Northern Ireland) Order 1995
	[Discharge of a Care Order
	Article 58(1) Children (Northern Ireland) Order 1995

The full name(s) of the child[ren]	Date(s) of birth

[The court orders	[that the child[ren] be placed in the care of
	Board/Trust]
[The court discharges	[the Care Order made by [this court] [the court]
	on]

Warning	While a Care Order is in force no person may cause the child[ren] to be known by a new surname or remove the child[ren] from the United Kingdom without the written consent of every person with parental responsibility for the child[ren] or the leave of the court.
	However, the Board or Trust, in whose care [a] [the] child[ren] [is] [are], may remove that child from the United Kingdom for a period of less than 1 month.
	It may be a criminal offence under the Child Abduction (Northern Ireland) Order 1985 to remove the child[ren] from the United Kingdom without the leave of the court.

Ordered by

on

FORM C28

IN THE MATTER OF THE CHILDREN
(NORTHERN IRELAND) ORDER 1995

[In the High Court of Justice in Northern Ireland]

[In the Divorce County Court for the
Division of   ]

[In the Family Care Centre at   ]

| Order | Interim Care Order |
| | Article 57 Children (Northern Ireland) Order 1995 |

| The full name(s) of the child[ren] | Date(s) of birth |

| The court orders | that the child[ren] be placed in the care of |
| | Board/Trust |

The order expires on

The court directs

Warning	While a Care Order is in force no person may cause the child[ren] to be known by a new surname or remove the child[ren] from the United Kingdom without the written consent of every person with parental responsibility for the child[ren] or the leave of the court.
	However, the Board or Trust, in whose care a child is, may remove that child from the United Kingdom for a period of less than 1 month.
	It may be a criminal offence under the Child Abduction (Northern Ireland) Order 1985 to remove the child[ren] from the United Kingdom without the leave of the court.

Ordered by

on

FORM C29

IN THE MATTER OF THE CHILDREN
(NORTHERN IRELAND) ORDER 1995

[In the High Court of Justice in Northern Ireland]

[In the Divorce County Court for the
Division of   ]

[In the Family Care Centre at   ]

Order	[Contact with a child in care Article 53(2) and (3) Children (Northern Ireland) Order 1995] [Authority to refuse contact with a child in care Article 53(4) Children (Northern Ireland) Order 1995]

The full name(s) of the child[ren]   Date(s) of birth

The authority

The court orders that   [there may be contact between the child[ren] and]

[the authority is authorised to refuse contact between the
child[ren] and]

[The contact is subject
to the following conditions]

[Notice   Any authority may refuse to allow the contact that would
otherwise be required by virtue of Article 53(1) of the
Children (Northern Ireland) Order 1995 or an order under
this section if (a) they are satisfied that it is necessary to
do so in order to safeguard or promote the welfare of the
child[ren]; and (b) the refusal (i) is decided upon as a
matter of urgency; and (ii) does not last for more than 7
days (Article 53(6) Children (Northern Ireland) Order
1995).]

Ordered by

on

IN THE MATTER OF THE CHILDREN
(NORTHERN IRELAND) ORDER 1995

[In the High Court of Justice in Northern Ireland]

[In the Divorce County Court for the
Division of   ]

[In the Family Care Centre at   ]

Order	[Supervision Order] Article 50 and Schedule 3 Children (Northern Ireland) Order 1995 [Interim Supervision Order] Article 57 and Schedule 3 Children (Northern Ireland) Order 1995

The full name(s) of the child[ren]	Date(s) of birth

The court orders

to supervise the child[ren]	[for a period of months from the date of this order]
	[for the interim period of]

The court directs

Ordered by _____

     on _____

FORM C31

IN THE MATTER OF THE CHILDREN
(NORTHERN IRELAND) ORDER 1995

[In the High Court of Justice in Northern Ireland]

[In the Divorce County Court for the
Division of   ]

[In the Family Care Centre at   ]

Order	[Substitution of a Supervision Order for a Care Order
	Article 58(4) Children (Northern Ireland) Order 1995]
	[Discharge] [Variation] of a Supervision Order
	Article 58(2) and (3) of the Children (Northern Ireland) Order 1995
	[Extension of a Supervision Order
	Paragraph 6(3) Schedule 3 Children (Northern Ireland) Order 1995]

The full name(s) of the child(ren)   Date(s) of birth

The court [substitutes]
[discharges] [varies]
[extends]   the [Supervision Order] [for the] [Care Order]

made by   [this court] [the

                                                    court]

on

The court orders

                    to supervise the child[ren].

The court directs

[This order ends on   ]

Ordered by   _____

        on

FORM C32

IN THE MATTER OF THE CHILDREN (NORTHERN IRELAND) ORDER 1995

[In the High Court of Justice in Northern Ireland]

[In the Divorce County Court for the
Division of   ]

[In the Family Care Centre at   ]

Order	Education Supervision Order Article 55 Children (Northern Ireland) Order 1995

The full name(s) of the child(ren)	Date(s) of birth

Warning	**A parent of the child[ren] may be guilty of an offence if he or she persistently fails to comply with a direction given by the supervisor under this order while it is in force** **(Paragraph 8 Schedule 4 Children (Northern Ireland) Order 1995)**

The court was satisfied	that the child[ren] [was] [were] of compulsory school age and [was] [were] not being properly educated.

The court orders

education and library board

to supervise the child[ren]	[for a period of 12 months beginning on the date of this order] [until the child[ren] [is] [are] no longer of compulsory school age].

Ordered by	_____
on	_____

IN THE MATTER OF THE CHILDREN
(NORTHERN IRELAND) ORDER 1995

[In the High Court of Justice in Northern Ireland]

[In the Divorce County Court for the
Division of   ]

[In the Family Care Centre at   ]

| Order | [Discharge of an Education Supervision Order
Paragraph 7 Schedule 4 Children (Northern Ireland) Order 1995]
[Extension of an Education Supervision Order
Paragraph 5 Schedule 4 Children (Northern Ireland) Order 1995] |

The full name(s) of the child(ren)	Date(s) of birth

The court [discharges]
[extends]   the Education Supervision Order

made by   [this court] [the

court]

on

requiring

education and library board to supervise the child[ren].

[The court directs   under Paragraph 7(2) Schedule 4 Children (Northern Ireland) Order 1995

Board [Trust] shall investigate the circumstances of the child[ren]]

[This order ends on   ]

Ordered by

on

FORM C34

IN THE MATTER OF THE CHILDREN
(NORTHERN IRELAND) ORDER 1995

[In the High Court of Justice in Northern Ireland]

[In the Divorce County Court for the
Division of   ]

[In the Family Care Centre at   ]

Order   Child Assessment Order
            Article 62 Children (Northern Ireland) Order 1995

The full name(s) of the child	Date of birth

The court orders	a [medical] [psychiatric] [
	] assessment of the child.

The court directs that
[the child is to be
assessed at]

[the child is to be
assessed by]

[the child may be kept
away from home and
stay at

from

to

While away from home, the child must be allowed contact
with   ]

the assessment is to
begin by

and last no more than   days from the date it begins.

Notice   Any person who is in a position to produce the child must
                do so to

                and must comply with the directions in this order.

Ordered by   _____

        on   _____

FORM C35

IN THE MATTER OF THE CHILDREN
(NORTHERN IRELAND) ORDER 1995

[In the High Court of Justice in Northern Ireland]

[In the Divorce County Court for the
Division of   ]

[In the Family Care Centre at   ]

Direction	To undertake an investigation
	Article 56 Children (Northern Ireland) Order 1995

The full name(s) of the child(ren)	Date(s) of birth

It appears to the court	that it may be appropriate for a Care or Supervision Order to be made in respect of the child[ren].
The court directs	the authority to investigate the circumstances of the child[ren].
[The court directs	copies of the following documents
	shall be served on the authority.]
Reporting the result	The authority must report to the court, in writing, under Article 56 of the Children (Northern Ireland) Order 1995

Ordered by _____

on _____

FORM C36

IN THE MATTER OF THE CHILDREN
(NORTHERN IRELAND) ORDER 1995

[In the High Court of Justice in Northern Ireland]

[In the Divorce County Court for the
Division of   ]

[In the Family Care Centre at   ]

Order   Family Assistance Order
             Article 16 Children (Northern Ireland) Order 1995

The full name(s) of the child(ren)   Date(s) of birth

The court orders   [an officer of

                                                 Board/Trust]
                        to be made available to advise, assist and, where
                        appropriate, befriend

[The court directs

This order ends on

    Notice This Order will have effect for 6 months from the date below, or such
    lesser period as specified.

Ordered by   _____

        on

184

FORM 37

IN THE MATTER OF THE CHILDREN
(NORTHERN IRELAND) ORDER 1995

[In the High Court of Justice in Northern Ireland]

[In the Divorce County Court for the
Division of   ]

[In the Family Care Centre at   ]

| Order | [Residence] [Contact] [Specific Issue] [Prohibited Steps] Order
Article 8 Children (Northern Ireland) Order 1995 |

The full name(s) of the child(ren)	Date(s) of birth

The court orders

Warning	Where a Residence Order is in force no person may cause the child[ren] to be known by a new surname or remove the child[ren] from the United Kingdom without the written consent of every person with parental responsibility for the child[ren] or the leave of the court.
	However, this does not prevent the removal of [a] child[ren], for a period of less than 1 month, by the person in whose favour the Residence Order is made (Article 13(1) and (2) Children (Northern Ireland) Order 1995).
	It may be a criminal offence under the Child Abduction (Northern Ireland) Order 1985 to remove the child[ren] from the United Kingdom without the leave of the court.
Notice	Any person with parental responsibility for [a] child[ren] may obtain advice on what can be done to prevent the issue of a passport to the child[ren]. They should write to The United Kingdom Passport Agency, Clive House, Petty France, LONDON, SW1H 9HD.

Ordered by   _____

          on

FORM C38

IN THE MATTER OF THE CHILDREN
(NORTHERN IRELAND) ORDER 1995

[In the High Court of Justice in Northern Ireland]

[In the Divorce County Court for the
Division of   ]

[In the Family Care Centre at   ]

Order   [Leave to change the surname by which a child is known
          Article 13(1) 52(7) Children (Northern Ireland) Order 1995]
          [Leave to remove a child from the United Kingdom
          Article 13(1) 52(7) Children (Northern Ireland) Order 1995]

          The full name(s) of the child(ren)   Date(s) of birth

The court grants leave to

[to change the child[ren]'s
surname to   ]

[and] [to remove the child[ren]]   from the United Kingdom

                                   [permanently] [until   ]

          Ordered by

              on

IN THE MATTER OF THE CHILDREN
(NORTHERN IRELAND) ORDER 1995

[In the High Court of Justice in Northern Ireland]

[In the Divorce County Court for the
Division of   ]

[In the Family Care Centre at   ]

| Order | [Parental Responsibility Order
Article 7(1) Children (Northern Ireland) Order 1995]
[Termination of a Parental Responsibility Order
Article 7(3) Children (Northern Ireland) Order 1995] |

| The full name(s) of the child(ren) | Date(s) of birth |

The court orders that

shall [no longer] have parental responsibility for the child[ren].

| **Notice** | A parental responsibility order can only end
(a) When the child reaches 18 years
(b) By order of the court made |

- on the application of any person who has parental responsibility
- with leave of the court on application of the child.

| Ordered by | _____ |
| on | _____ |

IN THE MATTER OF THE CHILDREN
(NORTHERN IRELAND) ORDER 1995

[In the High Court of Justice in Northern Ireland]

[In the Divorce County Court for the
Division of   ]

[In the Family Care Centre at   ]

Order   [Appointment of a guardian
             Article 159 Children (Northern Ireland) Order 1995]
             [Termination of the appointment of a guardian
             Article 163 Children (Northern Ireland) Order 1995]

The full name(s) of the child(ren)   Date(s) of birth

[The court appoints

to be the guardian of the child[ren].

This appointment will begin on

                                                                    ]

[The court orders that   the appointment of

as guardian of the child[ren] be terminated.]

Ordered by _____

on _____

IN THE MATTER OF THE CHILDREN
(NORTHERN IRELAND) ORDER 1995

[In the High Court of Justice in Northern Ireland]

[In the Divorce County Court for the
Division of   ]

[In the Family Care Centre at   ]

Order	[Making or refusing the appointment of a guardian ad litem Article 60 Children (Northern Ireland) Order 1995] [Termination of the appointment of a guardian ad litem Family Proceedings Rules (Northern Ireland) 1996: Rule 4.11(10)]

The full name(s) of the child(ren)	Date(s) of birth

The court [appoints] [refuses to appoint] [terminate the appointment of] [a[s] guardian ad litem] for the child[ren] in the proceedings

☐ for a Care Order or Supervision Order

☐ for discharge of a Care Order

☐ for variation or discharge of a Supervision Order

☐ for substitution of a Supervision Order for a Care Order

☐ for Contact, or Refusal of Contact, with a child in care

☐ for consideration of a Residence Order for a child in care

☐ under Article 33 Children (Northern Ireland) Order 1995

☐ under Paragraph 6(3) Schedule 3 Children (Northern Ireland) Order 1995

☐ under Part VI Children (Northern Ireland) Order 1995 (specify)

☐ where a Direction under Article 56(1) Children (Northern Ireland) Order 1995 has been made and the court [has made] [is considering] whether to make an [Interim Care Order] [Supervision Order]

☐ under Article 52(7) Children (Northern Ireland) Order 1995

☐ under Article 44 Children (Northern Ireland) Order 1995

☐ concerning an Appeal against a determination in any of the above proceedings

☐ other proceedings which are

The appointment shall continue until [   ] [terminated by the court]

Ordered by _____

on _____

FORM C42

IN THE MATTER OF THE CHILDREN
(NORTHERN IRELAND) ORDER 1995

[In the High Court of Justice in Northern Ireland]

[In the Divorce County Court for the
Division of   ]

[In the Family Care Centre at   ]

Order   [Appointment of a solicitor for a child
             Article 60(3) Children (Northern Ireland) Order 1995]
             [Refusal of the appointment of a solicitor
             Family Proceedings Rules (Northern Ireland) 1996: Rule 4.13(5) and (6)]
             [Termination of the appointment of a solicitor
             Family Proceedings Rules (Northern Ireland) 1996: Rule 4.13(3) and (4)]

The full name(s) of the child(ren)   Date(s) of birth

[The court is satisfied that the child[ren] [is] [are] not presently separately represented by a solicitor and

[● a guardian ad litem has not been appointed for the child[ren]; and]

[● the child[ren] [has] [have] sufficient understanding to instruct a solicitor and has expressed a wish to do so; and]

[● it would be in the interests of the child[ren] for [him] [her] [them] to be separately represented].

[The court orders that   [it refuses the appointment of a solicitor for the child[ren]]

                              [the appointment of]

                              [

                              of

                                                                              ]

                              [be appointed as solicitor for the child[ren]]

                              [as solicitor for the child[ren] be terminated]

Ordered by   _____

          on   _____

IN THE MATTER OF THE CHILDREN
(NORTHERN IRELAND) ORDER 1995

[In the High Court of Justice in Northern Ireland]

[In the Divorce County Court for the
Division of   ]

[In the Family Care Centre at   ]

Order   Transfer of proceedings to [the High Court] [the county court for the
             Division of   ] [family care centre at   ]
             [family proceedings court   ]

             The Children (Allocation of Proceedings) (Northern Ireland) Order 1995

The full name(s) of the child(ren)   Date(s) of birth

The court orders   that proceedings concerning the child[ren] be transferred to
                        the

                        [High Court] [the county court for the Division of
                                   ] [family care centre   ]
                        [family proceedings court   ]

        because

The next [Hearing]
[Directions Appointment]   is on   at   [am]   [pm]

                                at

Please address all
future correspondence to

        Ordered by   _____

                on

APPENDIX 2

CONTENTS OF PETITION

(Unless otherwise directed under Rule 2.4)

1. Every petition shall state:—

(*a*) the names of the parties to the marriage and the date and place of the marriage;

(*b*) the last address at which the parties to the marriage have lived together as husband and wife;

(*c*) where it is alleged that the court has jurisdiction based on domicile—

    (i) the country in which the petitioner is domiciled, and

    (ii) if that country is not Northern Ireland, the country in which the respondent is domiciled;

(*d*) where it is alleged that the court has jurisdiction based on habitual residence—

    (i) the country in which the petitioner has been habitually resident throughout the period of one year ending with the date of the presentation of the petition, or

    (ii) if the petitioner has not been habitually resident in Northern Ireland, the country in which the respondent has been habitually resident during that period,

with details in either case, including the addresses of the places of residence and the length of residence at each place;

(*e*) the occupation and residence of the petitioner and the respondent;

(*f*) whether there are any living children of the family and, if so—

    (i) the number of such children and the full names (including surname) of each and his date of birth or (if it be the case) that he is over 18 years of age; and

    (ii) in the case of each minor child over the age of 16, whether he is receiving instruction at an educational establishment or undergoing training for a trade, profession or vocation;

(*g*) whether (to the knowledge of the petitioner in the case of a husband's petition) any other child now living has been born to the wife during the marriage, and if so, the full names (including surname) of the child and his date of birth, or, if it be the case, that he is over 18 years of age;

(*h*) if it be the case, that there is a question whether a living child is a child of the family;

(*i*) where an application is being made for periodical payments or secured periodical payments for a child of the family,

    (i) whether the application is

        — for a stepchild;

        — in addition to child support maintenance; already payable under a Child Support Agency assessment;

        — to meet expenses arising from a child's disability;

        — to meet expenses incurred by a child being educated or trained for work;

        — on some other specified ground; or

(ii) that the child or the person with care of the child or the absent parent of the child is not habitually resident in the United Kingdom;

(j) whether or not there have been any applications under the Order of 1991 for a maintenance assessment in respect of any child of the family and if so

   (i) the date of any such application, and

   (ii) if available, details of the assessment made;

(k) whether or not there are or have been any other proceedings in any court in Northern Ireland or elsewhere with reference to the marriage or to any children of the family or between the petitioner and the respondent with reference to any property of either or both of them, and, if so—

   (i) the nature of the proceedings,

   (ii) the date and effect of any decree or order, and

   (iii) in the case of proceedings with reference to the marriage, whether there has been any resumption of cohabitation since the making of the decree or order;

(l) whether there are any proceedings continuing in any country outside Northern Ireland which relate to the marriage or are capable of affecting its validity of subsistence and, if so—

   (i) particulars of the proceedings, including the court in or tribunal or authority before which they were begun,

   (ii) the date when they were begun,

   (iii) the names of the parties,

   (iv) the date or expected date of any trial in the proceedings, and

   (v) such other facts as may be relevant to the question whether the proceedings on the petition should be stayed under Schedule 1 to the Order of 1978;

and such proceedings shall include any which are not instituted in a court of law in that country, if they are instituted before a tribunal or other authority having power under the law having effect there to determine questions of status, and shall be treated as continuing if they have been begun and have not been finally disposed of;

(m) where the fact on which the petition is based is 5 years' separation, whether any, and if so what, agreement or arrangement has been made or is proposed to be made between the parties for the support of the respondent or, as the case may be, the petitioner or any child of the family;

(n) in the case of a petition for divorce under Article 3(2)(e) of the Order of 1978 whether the petitioner proposes if a decree nisi is granted to make any financial provision for the respondent giving details of any proposal not mentioned under paragraph (k);

(o) in the case of a petition for divorce, that the marriage has broken down irretrievably;

(p) the fact alleged by the petitioner for the purposes of Article 3(2) of the Order of 1978 or, where the petition is not for divorce or judicial separation, the ground on which relief is sought, together in any case with brief particulars of the individual facts relied on but not the evidence by which they are to be proved;

(q) any further or other information required by such of the following paragraphs and by rule 88 as may be applicable.

2. A petition for a decree of nullity under Article 14(*e*) or (*f*) of the Order of 1978 shall state whether the petitioner was at the time of the marriage ignorant of the facts alleged.

3. A petition for a decree of presumption of death and dissolution of marriage shall state:—

(*a*) the last place at which the parties to the marriage cohabited;

(*b*) the circumstances in which the parties ceased to cohabit;

(*c*) the date when and the place where the respondent was last seen or heard of; and

(*d*) the steps which have been taken to trace the respondent.

4. Every petition shall conclude with—

(*a*) a prayer setting out particulars of the relief claimed, including any claim for costs and any application for ancillary relief which it is intended to claim;

(*b*) the names and addresses of the persons who are to be served with the petition, indicating if any of them is a person under disability;

(*c*) the petitioner's address for service, which, if the petitioner sues by a solicitor, shall be the solicitor's name or firm and address or, if the petitioner sues in person, shall be his place of residence as given under paragraph 1(*e*) above or, if no place of residence in Northern Ireland is given, the address to which documents for him may be delivered or sent.

NOTICES AND RESPONDENTS

(i)	(ii)	(iii)	(iv)
Provision under which proceedings brought	*Minimum number of days prior to hearing or directions appointment for service under rule 4.5(1)(b)*	*Respondents*	*Persons to whom notice is to be given*
All applications	See separate entries below	Subject to separate entries below:	Subject to separate entries below:
		every person whom the applicant believes to have parental responsibility for the child;	any authority providing accommodation for the child;
		where the child is the subject of a care order, every person whom the applicant believes to have had parental responsibility immediately prior to the making of the care order;	persons who are caring for the child at the time when the proceedings are commenced;
		in the case of an application to extend, vary or discharge an order, the parties to the proceedings leading to the order which it is sought to have extended, varied or discharged;	in the case of proceedings brought in respect of a child who is alleged to be staying in a refuge which is certificated under Article 70(1) or (2), the person who is providing the refuge.
		in the case of specified proceedings, the child.	
Article 7(1)(a), 7(4), 8, 13(1), 16(6), 33(1), 52(7), 159(1), 163(1), Schedule 1, Paragraphs 10(3) and 12(4) of Schedule 8	14 days	As for "all applications" above, and:	As for "all applications" above, and:
		in the case of proceedings under Schedule 1, those persons whom the applicant believes to be interested in or affected by proceedings;	in the case of an application for an Article 8 order, every person whom applicant believes—
		in the case of an application under paragraph 10(3)(b) or 12(4) of Schedule 8, any person, other than the child, named in the order	(i) to be named in a court order with respect to the same child, which has not ceased to have effect,
			(ii) to be a party to pending proceedings

195

(i)	(ii)	(iii)	(iv)
Provision under which proceedings brought	*Minimum number of days prior to hearing or directions appointment for service under rule 4.5(1)(b)*	*Respondents*	*Persons to whom notice is to be given*
		or directions which it is sought to discharge or vary.	in respect of the same child, or
			(iii) to be a person with whom the child has lived for at least 3 years prior to the application,
			unless, in a case to which (i) or (ii) applies, the applicant believes that the court order or pending proceedings are not relevant to the application;
			in the case of an application under Article 33(1), the parties to the proceedings leading to the care order;
			in the case of an application under Article 159(1), the father of the child if he does not have parental responsibility.
Article 55(1), 58(1), 58(2), 58(3), 58(4), 62(1), Paragraph 6(3) of Schedule 3, Paragraphs 5(2) and 7(1) of Schedule 4	7 days	As for "all applications" above, and: in the case of an application under Article 58(2) or (3), the supervisor; in the case of proceedings under paragraph 7(1) of Schedule 4, the education and library board concerned; in the case of proceedings under Article 55 or paragraph 5(2) or 7(1) of Schedule 4, the child.	As for "all applications" above, and: in the case of an application for an order under Article 62(1)— (i) every person whom the applicant believes to be a parent of the child, (ii) every person whom the applicant believes to be caring for the child, (iii) every person in whose favour a contact order is in force with respect to the child, and

196

(i) *Provision under which proceedings brought*	(ii) *Minimum number of days prior to hearing or directions appointment for service under rule 4.5(1)(b)*	(iii) *Respondents*	(iv) *Persons to whom notice is to be given*
			(iv) every person who is allowed to have contact with the child by virtue of an order under Article 53.
Article 50, 53(2), 53(3), 53(4), 53(9) or 57(8)(*b*)	3 days	As for "all applications" above, and: in the case of an application under Article 53, the person whose contact with the child is the subject of the application.	As for "all applications" above, and: in the case of an application under Article 50— (i) every person whom the applicant believes to be a party to pending relevant proceedings in respect of the same child, and (ii) every person whom the applicant believes to be a parent without parental responsibility for the child.
Article 62(12)	2 days	As for "all applications" above.	Those of the persons referred to in Article 62(11)(*a*) to (*e*) who were not party to the application for the order which it is sought to have varied or discharged.
Article 44, 63(1), 63(9)(*b*), 64(3), 64(7), 67(9), 69(1), 178(1)	1 day	As for "all applications" above, and: in the case of an application under Article 63(9)(*b*)— (i) the parties to the application for the order in respect of which it is sought to vary the directions; (ii) any person who was caring for the child	Except for applications under Article 178(1), as for "all applications" above, and: in the case of an application under Article 63(1), every person whom the applicant believes to be a parent of the child; in the case of an application under Article 63(9)(*b*)—

(i)	(ii)	(iii)	(iv)
Provision under which proceedings brought	*Minimum number of days prior to hearing or directions appointment for service under rule 4.5(1)(b)*	*Respondents*	*Persons to whom notice is to be given*
		prior to the making of the order, and (iii) any person whose contact with the child is affected by the direction which it is sought to have varied;	(i) the authority in whose area the child is living, and (ii) any person whom the applicant believes to be affected by the direction which it is sought to have varied;
		in the case of an application under Article 69, the person whom the applicant alleges to have effected or to have been or to be responsible for the taking or keeping of the child.	in the case of an application under Article 178(1), the person referred to in Article 178(1) and any person preventing or likely to prevent such a person from exercising powers under enactments mentioned in paragraph (6) of that Article.

EXPLANATORY NOTE

(This note is not part of the Rules.)

These rules which apply to proceedings in the High Court and county courts provide for applications

— under the Matrimonial Causes (Northern Ireland) Order 1978 and under Article 31 (declaration as to martial status), 41 (transfer of tenancy upon divorce) and Part IV (financial relief after overseas divorce) of the Matrimonial and Family Proceedings (Northern Ireland) Order 1989, revoking and replacing the Matrimonial Causes Rules (Northern Ireland) 1981 [S.R. 1981 No. 184 as amended by S.R. 1989 No. 246 and S.R. 1993 No. 134]; and

— under the Children (Northern Ireland) Order 1995.

Printed in the United Kingdom for the
Controller of Her Majesty's Stationery Office
being the Officer appointed to print the
Measures of the Northern Ireland Assembly and
published by Her Majesty's Stationery Office

Dd. 310076. C12. 8/96. Gp. 130. 14567.

£15·65